THE ESSENTIAL BOOK OF
SUCCULENTS

A Guide to the 250 Best Varieties for Beginners

KENTARO KURODA

TUTTLE Publishing

Tokyo | Rutland, Vermont | Singapore

CONTENTS

PART 1

Characteristics and Care Guidelines for Popular Varieties

SPECIAL FEATURES

What are Succulents?

Everyone loves succulents for their cute forms and plump, fleshy leaves. They come in various shapes and sizes—chubby ones, fuzzy ones, and even spiky ones. Their diverse appearances keep us fascinated.

One of the many appealing things about succulents is that they can thrive with minimal water and in small pots. This makes them perfect for enjoying in tight spaces like balconies, windowsills, or tabletops. It's no wonder that many people find themselves collecting these charming plants. And since most succulents grow slowly, taking care of them is not too demanding.

If you've ever thought about growing succulents but felt overwhelmed by the sheer variety available, you're not alone. To help you with this, our book carefully selects and introduces twenty genera that are visually appealing, easy to care for, and readily available.

Start by buying one succulent that really appeals to you. The general rule is to place them in a well-lit area with good air circulation and water them sparingly. With an understanding of the fundamental care guidelines, anyone can successfully nurture these lovely plants. It's so easy to add refreshing greenery to your living space!

Why not use this book as a reference and try growing some unique and charming succulents? What are succulents, you ask? In this book, Ken Kuroda will guide you through all the basics.

Ways to Enjoy Succulents

Enjoy Watching Them Grow

Succulent plants are relatively easy to care for, making them a great choice for beginners or those who aren't keen on frequent maintenance. You can appreciate the changing seasons and the gradual growth of these plants, and savor the joy of nurturing them. Many succulents come from dry regions like South Africa and Central South America, giving them unique and captivating appearances. Despite their slow growth, succulents can surprise you with stunning, vibrant flowers that seem to bloom out of nowhere, similar to cacti. Some, like Lithops, produce new leaves that emerge from cracks in their stone-

The top two plants are both cacti. The densely packed flower bud in the top left eventually grows a long stem and blooms into beautiful flowers. The bottom left shows the process of Lithops shedding its old leaves. The bottom right depicts a Kalanchoe with numerous offshoots attached along the edge of its leaves.

like foliage before shedding their old ones. Kalanchoe species sometimes sprout tiny leaves along the edges of their larger leaves, creating a growth pattern that's fascinating and enjoyable to observe.

Enjoy Propagating Them

Succulent plants are often robust and have strong vitality, making them easy to propagate. One way is through leaf propagation. Plants with chubby leaves like Echeveria and Kalanchoe can produce small offsets from the base of a dried leaf when placed in a dry location. This process showcases their strong life force, and observing these miniature offspring can be quite gratifying. You can also easily propagate succulents through division or stem cuttings, making it effortless to cultivate many of your favorite varieties.

The photo shows the process of leaf propagation. By placing leaves of succulents like Echeveria, Kalanchoe, or Graptopetalum on dry soil, tiny offsets will emerge and take root. It's truly fascinating to witness the mystery of life, as a robust plant can grow from just a single leaf.

Three Growth Types

Succulent plants can be broadly categorized into three types based on their growth cycles. These differences in growth types are a reflection of their native environmental conditions. Being aware of this can help you cultivate them harmoniously. Let's get started by understanding the characteristics and key points of each growth type.

SPRING-FALL TYPE

This type of succulent grows during spring and fall, preferring mild and warm climates. The typical optimal growing temperature range is around 50–77°F (10–25°C). During winter and summer, they enter a semi-dormant state with slowed growth. During this period, it's best to reduce watering. In the summer, provide shade, ensure good airflow, and be cautious of overwatering. In the winter, take measures to protect them from the cold, such as bringing them indoors. There are many varieties within this type that are suitable for beginners and relatively easy to cultivate.

Sedum (→ p.14)

Echeveria (→ p.18)

Haworthia (→ p.22)

Cotyledon (→ p.46)

Graptopetalum (→ p.48)

Pachyphytum (→ p.50)

SUMMER TYPE

This type of succulent is relatively tolerant of heat and grows during periods of rising temperatures, typically from spring to fall. However, growth may slow down during extremely hot periods. The ideal temperature range for growth is around 60–86°F (15–30°C). Growth starts to decline as temperatures drop in the fall, and they go dormant in winter. High humidity and intense sunlight during summer can cause damage, so it's important to ensure good airflow and take measures against leaf scorch. During winter, reduce watering and provide adequate protection against the cold.

Kalanchoe (→ p.26)

Euphorbia (→ p.30)

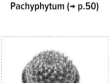

Cactus (→ p.32)

Agave (→ p.34)

Aloe (→ p.36)

WINTER/COLD-HARDY TYPE

This type of succulent is relatively resilient to cold temperatures and grows during the cooler periods. They are not fond of heat and humidity. The best temperature range for growth is around 40–68°F (5–20°C). During summer, they go dormant, so be sure to ensure good airflow and reduce watering. They typically begin growing again in the fall. Winter growth is gradual, so be sure to protect them from temperatures below 41°F (5°C). In spring, growth again becomes active. There are relatively fewer varieties within the cold-hardy type.

Lithops (→ p.38)

Some Senecio species (→ p.54)

Othonna (→ p.54)

Points to Consider When Selecting Succulents

When looking at the display, it's easy to be tempted by everything you see. First, think about where you want to place the plants and how much care you can put into them. Imagine yourself caring for them, then choose something that both excites you and feels workable.

1 Think about where you want to place them

Do you want to grow them outdoors or indoors? Visualize where you want to place them in your home. This will determine which varieties to choose. Generally, succulents thrive outdoors, but Haworthia and Rhipsalis can thrive indoors with some shade. For indoor plants, ensure they have good sunlight and airflow and avoid overwatering. If you can provide these conditions, cacti are also suitable.

2 Consider the type of plants you want to display

Next, think about the types of plants, pot sizes, and aesthetics you prefer. Whether you want to display lots of cute small sedums, impressive spiky aloes, or elegant trailing Rhipsalis in your living room, visualize it specifically. Finding pots in sizes and colors that complement the plants will enhance their appeal and add to the excitement.

3 Know how they grow

Once you've narrowed down your choices, it's important to understand how each type of succulent grows. Different species have different growth rates. Fast-growing sedums require frequent pruning, suitable for those who enjoy gardening. On the other hand, if you prefer low-maintenance, slow-growing succulents like cacti might be perfect. Consider whether they spread horizontally or grow vertically and choose accordingly to balance with the placement.

Things to consider when choosing plants

1 Is it elongated?
Avoid plants with elongated stems that appear weak and frail, indicating insufficient sunlight.

2 Is it diseased?
Check the leaves and stems for signs of discoloration, holes, or a powdery appearance, indicating disease or pests.

3 Is it sunburned?
Sunburn can occur when exposed to intense sunlight, leading to discoloration and sometimes permanent damage or rot. Avoid sunburned plants.

4 Is it compact?
Choose plants with compact, sturdy growth and well-established roots. Avoid plants with loose or wobbly roots.

5 Is the color vibrant?
Select plants with vibrant leaf and stem colors. Pale or dull colors suggest insufficient sunlight. Avoid plants with powdery residue, as this indicates poor maintenance.

6 Is it the right time to buy?
The best time to purchase succulents is during their growing season, typically in spring or fall. This allows for immediate repotting and ensures optimal growth conditions.

After Purchasing Your Succulents

Once you've purchased your favorite succulent plants, your green life journey begins. Start by repotting them into your favorite pots and taking care of them daily. Observing them closely, watering appropriately, and encouraging their growth will help them thrive.

1   Pots and Tools

Choosing pots that match your succulent plants adds to the joy of growing them. It's essential to select pots that not only fit your aesthetic preferences but also consider factors like material and drainage holes. The amount and timing of watering vary depending on the pot. For beginners, porous and evaporative terracotta pots are recommended. Here are some tools you might want to have on hand for repotting and regular care:

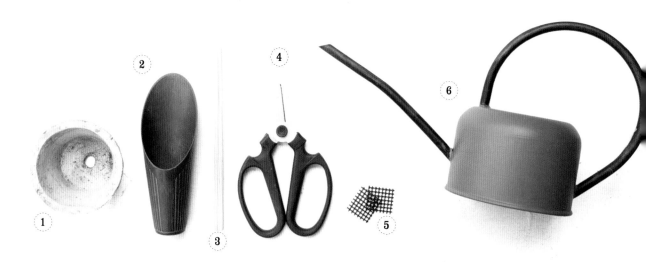

1   Pots

Terracotta or moss pots with drainage holes allow for better airflow and drainage, which is crucial for succulents. If your chosen pot doesn't have drainage holes, consider drilling some in the bottom.

2   Potting soil

Tools for filling soil into pots during repotting. Choose sizes that are convenient for you. If you don't have dedicated tools, you can use empty plastic pots.

3   Trowel or chopsticks

Handy for evenly distributing soil during repotting. For small pots, a bamboo stick can suffice. Lightly tapping the soil with it helps to settle it in.

4   Gardening scissors

Used for trimming unnecessary leaves, stems, or roots, and for tidying overgrown stems. Opt for thin-bladed, long-handled scissors that won't damage the plants. Remember to disinfect them with alcohol after use.

5   Pot mesh

Placed over the drainage holes to prevent soil from washing out and pests from entering during repotting. They are reusable and made of plastic.

6   Watering can

Used for watering. Narrow-mouthed cans allow for targeted watering without splashing onto leaves or stems, making them easier to use, especially in tight spaces.

2 Soils

For succulent plants, soil is like their "home." To ensure they grow healthy, it's important to provide them with a suitable environment. A hint for this can be found in their natural habitat. Since they typically grow in dry regions like deserts, they prefer well-draining soil compared to regular garden plants. For beginners, commercially available succulent soil mixes are convenient and recommended. If you want your plants to grow quickly and robustly, a blend of akadama soil is suitable. This blend consists of 40% akadama soil, 20% humus, 20% perlite, and 10% each of charcoal and vermiculite.

Succulent soil mix

Commercially available succulent soil mixes are formulated with small particles of perlite to improve drainage. This soil mix is suitable for succulents as it provides good drainage, making it forgiving for beginners who might tend to overwater.

Akadama soil

Akadama soil is sieved volcanic red soil sold in various sizes, primarily used for succulent plant cultivation in its smaller particle form. It is slightly acidic and offers good aeration, moisture retention, and fertility. It is typically blended with humus and perlite.

Regular potting soil

Commercially available potting soil for regular plants. However, as it retains too much water for succulents, mix it with 40% small particle akadama soil to improve drainage.

Bottom layer stones

Placing stones at the bottom of the pot improves drainage and aeration, preventing root rot. As a general rule, fill about one-fifth of the pot with stones, but for deeper pots, adding more is beneficial. Use small particles of perlite or similar material if mixing with soil.

3 Planting in Pots

Prepare a pot one size larger than the one the succulent plant came in. Place the pot mesh followed by bottom layer stones, then add a small amount of soil. Gently loosen the roots of the plant from its original pot and plant it in the new pot. This ensures better integration with the new soil. Hold the plant steady with one hand to prevent it from tipping over while adding more soil. Avoid covering the base of the plant with new soil, as this can suffocate it. Water generously until water flows out from the bottom of the pot.

Planting at the same level as the rim of the pot can cause soil to spill over during watering. To prevent this, plant the succulent slightly below the rim, creating a water space about ⅜" (1cm) below the pot's edge.

4 Daily Care

During the active growth periods, use a watering can with a wide spout to give the entire plant a thorough shower. If there's a saucer under the pot, discard any excess water that collects.

Watering

The fundamental principle of watering is to wait until the soil is completely dry before watering again. Overwatering can lead to root rot. During the active growth periods in spring and fall, water generously throughout the plant. From the start of the rainy season to mid-September when the lingering heat of summer persists, reduce watering significantly to allow the plants to rest. During hot weather, water the soil directly without wetting the leaves. Be cautious during the extreme cold of December to February, as moist soil at night may freeze, so pay close attention. Gradually increase watering from March onwards. In summer, avoid watering during the hot daytime and instead water in the evening. During extreme cold, water during the day to avoid freezing temperatures at night.

Placement

The ideal environment for succulents is a location with long hours of sunlight and good airflow. Insufficient sunlight and poor airflow can result in poor leaf color and elongation. During spring, ensure they receive ample sunlight outdoors. Prolonged rainfall can cause root rot, so during the rainy season, manage them under eaves where they're protected from rain. Japan's hot and humid summers with intense sunlight are challenging for succulents. Provide shade using shade nets or move them to a cool, semi-shaded area to let them rest. From late September, gradually expose them to sunlight again, and from October, place them in a sunny and well-ventilated location. During winter, avoid cold winds and frost. Move them indoors to a sunny location that maintains a temperature above 41°F (5°C).

Locations with good sunlight and airflow, protected from direct rainfall by roofs or eaves, also shield from intense summer sunlight. Shelves offer better airflow than placing them directly on the ground.

Fertilization

Succulents naturally grow in nutrient-poor environments like gravel or desert soils, so they don't require much fertilizer. Additionally, fertilizing during summer or winter semi-dormant or dormant periods may damage them. Some varieties won't exhibit vibrant colors if over-fertilized. Fertilize only during active growth periods. There's initial fertilization when planting or repotting and supplemental fertilization to promote growth. Use slow-release fertilizer for initial fertilization, but if using pre-fertilized commercial soil, you may not need to mix it in. For supplemental fertilization, dilute liquid fertilizer more than recommended and apply monthly during the active growth period. This will enhance leaf color as well.

Liquid fertilizers (left) have an immediate effect. Use them once a month during the growing season. Slow-release fertilizers (right) have a gradual and lasting effect, and are great for initial fertilization.
*Always follow manufacturer directions and protect your eyes, skin, and air passages.

PART 1

Characteristics and
Care Guidelines for
Popular Varieties

Sedum

BASIC DATA

Scientific name: **Sedum**
Family: **Crassulaceae**
Genus: **Sedum**
Also known as: **Stonecrop, Crassula**
Native to: **Various regions around the world**
Growth type: **Spring-fall type**
Propagation: **Division, stem cuttings, leaf cuttings**

With variations in leaf shape, size, color, and growth habits, Sedums offer a diverse range of characteristics. Starting from the top right and moving clockwise, there's the *burrito* which grows in clusters and trails downward, the *rubrotinctum* with vibrant foliage, the *makinoi f. variegata* with striking white-edged small leaves, the fluffy *versadense*, *pachyphyllum*, 'Aurea', and the upright 'Golden Glow'.

Sedum is the largest genus in the Crassulaceae family, with over 400 species distributed widely across the globe. It includes varieties with small, chubby leaves clustered together, those forming rosettes, trailing varieties, and even tree-like forms with upright stems. While most varieties available domestically are cold-hardy, they tend to struggle in hot and humid conditions. Some varieties native or naturalized in Japan are well-known as "perennial plants," appreciated for their cold tolerance and suitability for ground cover in open spaces. They grow quickly, and depending on the variety, can be easily propagated through division, stem cuttings, or leaf cuttings.

Characteristics of Sedums

Creeping type: Spreads horizontally

Characterized by its tendency to spread across the ground by densely packing small leaves. It creates a carpet-like effect. Varieties like *makinoi* on the right belong to this type, often indicated by names including Stonecrop. Examples include *dasyphyllum var. alternum* at the bottom and *makinoi* 'Aurea' on the top left.

Upright, bushy type: Grows upward into bushes

Some Sedums, like *pachyphyllum* on the left and *lucidum* on the right, have stems that stand upright. As they grow, lower leaves drop off, leaving foliage only on the upper parts, giving them a bushy appearance. They make lovely arrangements in mixed plantings, utilizing the movement of their stems.

Cute little flowers blooming from spring to fall

They produce small flower buds densely packed at the tips of elongated flower stalks. Flowering times vary depending on the variety, typically from March to November. These charming star-shaped flowers come in various colors, predominantly yellow and white, with some varieties having red hues as well. The photo shows *mexicanum*.

Enjoy their fall foliage from fall to early spring

As temperatures drop, the leaves gradually turn pink or red, becoming vividly colored in the dead of winter. Representative varieties include *rubrotinctum* and "Aurora." As spring approaches and temperatures rise, the foliage gradually loses its red coloration, returning to its original green or grayish hue.

Cultivation Calendar

	JAN	FEB	MAR	APR	MAY	JUN	JUL	AUG	SEP	OCT	NOV	DEC
Growth Period (Growing Season / Dormant Period)	Partial dormancy		Growing season				Slow growth period	Dormant period	Growing season			
Flowering												
Transplanting, Dividing, Propagation by Cutting, Leaf Cuttings												
Fertilizer												

Daily Care

Watering and Fertilizing

During the growing seasons of spring and fall, water generously when the soil surface is dry. From mid-July to mid-September, during the slow growth period to dormancy, reduce watering to allow the soil to dry slightly. Sedums dislike excessive moisture in hot weather. Fertilize with diluted liquid fertilizer once a month to promote growth. When transplanting, mix slow-release fertilizer into the soil as a base fertilizer.

Placement

During spring to fall, place in a sunny and well-ventilated area. During the rainy season and midsummer, it's best to keep them under eaves to avoid rain. In winter, place them under a sunny eave. For varieties sensitive to cold, consider moving them indoors to a sunny location or using a simple frame to protect them from cold winds and frost.

Transplanting and Pruning

Due to their rapid growth, transplant once a year. Gently loosen the root ball and remove excess soil, then plant in fresh potting soil mixed with base fertilizer. During transplanting, if the plant appears leggy, it's acceptable to trim and shape it lower.

Propagation

Creeping types like perennial plants are suitable for division, while bushy types are suitable for stem cuttings. Stems or leaves trimmed during transplanting can be used for stem or leaf cuttings. Especially for fast-growing varieties like perennial plants, division can be done as needed during the growing season to propagate them.

Division

For creeping types (like the 'Aurea' pictured below), when the plant has spread to fill the pot, it's time for division and transplanting. The suitable periods are during the growing seasons of spring and fall. Because of their fast growth, division can be done twice a year as needed.

1 Carefully remove the plant from the pot along with its root ball. Sedum roots are delicate, so gently loosen them with your fingers and remove excess soil. Slowly divide the roots.

2 Next, separate the upper stems and leaves by gently untangling them with your thumb. Be careful not to tear the stems or leaves by applying too much force.

3 You can remove the bottom third of the root ball. Place a bit of fresh potting soil in the bottom of the new pot and plant, leaving space for watering.

4 Prepare another pot and plant the remaining divisions. Water immediately after planting.

Pruning / Propagation by Stem Cuttings

For types that grow upright and become bushy (pictured: Sedum pachyphyllum Rose), after several years of growth, the lower leaves may fall off and the plant may become leggy. Prune and propagate by stem cuttings. New shoots will emerge from the remaining base of the plant.

BEFORE   AFTER

1 Remove any dead leaves. Leave the new shoots at the base of the plant and cut back the leggy stems from the base.

2 Use the cut-off tips for stem cuttings. Cut the stem into ⅞–1⅛" (2–3cm) lengths and let the cut ends dry in the shade for about 1 week to 10 days.

3 Insert the cuttings into fresh potting soil. Keep them in bright shade and they should root within 3–4 weeks. Once roots have formed, begin watering.

4 Also, transplant the parent plant left in the pot from step 2. Gently remove the root ball, loosen it, and remove old roots and soil.

5 Plant the cuttings from step 4 into the pot with fresh potting soil, leaving space for watering.

6 Water immediately after planting.

Echeveria

BASIC DATA

Scientific Name: **Echeveria**
Family: **Crassulaceae**
Genus: **Echeveria**
Origin: **Mexico, Central and South America**
Growth Type: **Spring-Fall type**
Propagation: **Stem cuttings, leaf cuttings**

From top left, we have the wine-red 'Autumn Flame', 'Lola', *lilacina* with a powdery white coating, middle left *subsessilis*, 'Arctic Ice', 'Neon Breakers' with frilly leaves, bottom left 'Mallow', 'Ginbugen', 'Perle von Nurnberg' which turns more purple-pink in colder weather, and the clumping 'Ilia' that pups easily.
* For varieties see pages 86–89

With leaves spreading in a rosette shape, this genus is popular for its beauty. There are varieties ranging from small types with about 1⅛" (3cm) in diameter to large ones exceeding 12" (30cm), with diverse leaf colors including shades of green, red, black, blue, and purple. As the temperature drops in fall, the leaves gradually begin to turn red, offering a vibrant display. By spring and with warmer weather, the red leaves fade gradually back to their original colors, but some varieties produce delicate flowers from between the leaves until summer. Numerous hybrids and cultivars have been developed, making Echeveria a diverse succulent plant.

Characteristics of Echeveria

Beautiful rosette-shaped leaves

The leaves of Echeveria all form rosette shapes, radiating from the center. The photo shows 'Powder Blue'. Some types readily produce offsets at the base, forming clusters.

Bell-shaped flowers bloom from spring to summer

Long flower stalks emerge from the base, bearing several small flowers in shades of orange or pink at the tips. The sight of them blooming slightly drooped is charming. However, some varieties weaken after flowering, so it's advisable to trim the flower buds early. The photo shows 'Deresina'.

Glossy fall to spring foliage

While the intensity of color varies among varieties, the vibrancy of the foliage is captivating. Full coloration typically starts in late November, but exposing them to ample sunlight from September and reducing fertilizer can enhance their beauty. The left photo shows *agavoides* (left) and 'Prism'.

Some leaves are covered in white powder

The white powder is actually fructose produced by the plant itself. It protects the leaves from strong sunlight in their native habitat and helps prevent water loss through transpiration. Since touching it can mar its beauty, it's best not to touch it. The photo shows *lilacina*.

Cultivation Calendar

	JAN	FEB	MAR	APR	MAY	JUN	JUL	AUG	SEP	OCT	NOV	DEC
Growth Period (Growing Season / Dormant Period)	Dormant period		Growing season				Semi-dormant period		Growing season			Slow growth period
Flowering				●————————————●								
Transplanting, Dividing, Propagation by Cutting, Leaf Cuttings			●————————●							●————————●		
Fertilizer			●————————●							●————————●		

Daily Care

Watering and Fertilizing

During the spring and fall growth periods, water generously when the soil surface dries out. During the rainy season to summer, be cautious of over-humid conditions and allow the soil to dry slightly. Be careful not to let water accumulate in the center of the rosette as it can damage the growth point. Fertilize with slow-release or liquid fertilizer at the beginning of the growing season. Avoid excessive fertilization in fall to prevent hindering beautiful fall colors.

Placement

Manage the plants in a sunny and well-ventilated area like a balcony. Avoid exposing them to prolonged rain by placing them under eaves. In midsummer, provide partial shade or use shading to reduce intense sunlight. By the time frost arrives, either place them in a simple frame outdoors where they can avoid cold winds or manage them indoors.

Repotting and Pruning

The ideal time for repotting is at the beginning of the growing season. Gently loosen the root ball and remove some soil. Plant it in well-draining new potting soil mixed with slow-release fertilizer as a base fertilizer. Be careful not to touch the white powder covering the leaves as much as possible. If the plant becomes too tall, it's acceptable to trim it back and reshape it.

Propagation

Echeveria can be propagated by stem cuttings and leaf cuttings. Cuttings from pruning can be used for stem cuttings. Leaves that come off easily can be used for leaf cuttings. Place them on dry soil in a bright shade for 3 to 4 weeks until roots develop. Water once every 4 to 5 days after roots appear. Once new shoots start to grow, transplant them into pots.

Do not let water accumulate between the leaves

After watering, be cautious not to let water droplets accumulate between the leaves, especially during summer, as it can damage the leaves or lead to diseases. Gently tilt the pot to remove excess water droplets.

Propagation through leaf cuttings

Place the leaves on top of dry soil in a bright shade. Roots will grow from the base of the leaf, and eventually, new shoots will emerge. The photo shows leaf cuttings taken in April, approximately two months later. It's lovely to see them growing into shapes similar to the parent plant, albeit smaller.

Pruning and Stem Cutting

As Echeveria grows, old outer leaves will wither. Here's how to prune and propagate while maintaining the rosette shape.

BEFORE

AFTER

1

Gently remove the withered outer leaves by hand. They should come off easily when pulled or moved gently sideways.

2

All withered leaves removed, revealing a stem-like structure.

3

Use scissors to cut the stem slightly above the base. The cut upper part becomes the cutting.

4

It's easier to insert the stem into the soil when it's ⅞–1⅛" (2–3cm) long, so remove the lower leaves by hand. Let the cut end dry in the shade for about a week.

5

Insert the stem straight into fresh potting soil (used in a dry state). It will root in 2–3 weeks. Start watering after rooting begins.

6

Place the leaves taken in step 4 slightly apart on dry potting soil and keep them in bright shade. Do not water. Roots will develop in 3–4 weeks, and new shoots will start to emerge, as per the bottom right photo on page 20.

Haworthia

Scientific Name: **Haworthia**
Family: **Asphodelaceae**
Genus: **Haworthia**
Also known as: **Crystal Plant, Jewel of the Desert**
Origin: **South Africa**
Growth Type: **Spring-Fall type**
Propagation: **Division, leaf cuttings**

From the top left, the hybrid 'Mirror Ball' with beautiful transparent windows, *obtusa* 'Murasaki Obtusa' × *venusta* adorned with short white hairs. From the middle left, *picta* with white spots on the windows, *obtusa*. From the bottom left, 'Black Splendens', and *cuspidata*, with triangular leaves forming star-shaped rosettes.
* For varieties see pages 90–91

In its native habitat of South Africa, Haworthia quietly inhabits the shade of rocks, bushes, and at the base of trees, thus it is sensitive to direct sunlight and prefers bright indoor windowsills. They are broadly categorized into the soft-leaved "soft-leaf" types and the hard-leaved "hard-leaf" types. Both types grow in rosette forms, radiating outward, which is both beautiful and popular. The differences in patterns on the leaves, including the overall pattern and the transparency of the "windows" at the leaf tips, offer unique characteristics to each variety. Even larger specimens typically have a diameter of around 6" (15cm). As offsets grow around the parent plant, they can be divided to propagate new plants. Crossbreeding to create new horticultural varieties is also common.

Characteristics of Haworthia

Leaves with semi-transparent "windows" at the tips

One type of "soft-leaf" variety features semi-transparent areas called "windows" at the tips of their leaves. They evolved this way in their native habitat to efficiently capture light while hiding in shadows, creating this unique shape. They gleam when illuminated. Pictured is *obtusa*.

"Ruffled" edges adorn the leaves

Fine teeth (serrations) along the edges of the leaves extend into slender threads, resembling white lace. This is another type of "soft-leaf" variety. The photo shows *borsii × var. aranea*.

Flowers bloom in spring to early summer and fall to winter

Long, slender flower stalks emerge from the base, bearing delicate single flowers. Flower colors range from white to pink. As the plant weakens after flowering, once several flowers have bloomed, trim the stalk to about 1⅛" (3cm) from the base. When the stalk is completely dried, pull it out.

Leaves with sharp, hard tips

The "hard-leaf" varieties are characterized by their elongated, sharp appearance. They often feature dots or stripes on the leaves. The photo shows *attentuate* (left) with vivid green leaves and white dashed patterns, and *reinwardtii var. archibaldiae* with dark green leaves adorned with white dots.

Cultivation Calendar

	JAN	FEB	MAR	APR	MAY	JUN	JUL	AUG	SEP	OCT	NOV	DEC
Growth Period (Growing Season / Dormant Period)	Semi-dormant period		Growing period				Semi-dormant period		Growing period			
Flowering				○────────	────────○				○────	────	────○	
Transplanting, Dividing, Propagation by Cutting, Leaf Cuttings				○────	────○				○────	────○		
Fertilizer				○────	────○				○────	────○		

Daily Care

Watering and Fertilizing

During the growing period, water generously when the surface of the soil dries out. Since they generally prefer water, be careful not to let them dry out too much. However, be more conservative with watering during summer and winter. Fertilize with a diluted liquid fertilizer about once a month. When repotting, it's beneficial to mix in slow-release fertilizer as a base fertilizer.

Placement

Outdoors in a balcony with good sunlight exposure and ventilation is ideal. They generally prefer sunlight but dislike intense light. From around May, place them in partial shade for half a day to prevent leaf scorch. They can also be grown indoors near windows. In winter, when frost starts to appear, either place them in a sheltered area with a makeshift frame to avoid cold winds or manage them indoors. They are relatively tolerant of cold temperatures but beware of freezing.

Repotting

Repotting should be done in the early stages of the growing period. Since offsets develop and grow in clusters, you can divide them during repotting. Leave the healthy white roots intact, remove the brown old roots, and repot.

Propagation

They can be propagated through division and leaf cuttings. When dividing, gently remove the soil, being careful not to damage the roots. Avoid dividing too forcefully. For leaf cuttings, be sure to include the base of the leaf attached to the stem. Applying rooting hormone to the cut end and allowing it to dry is beneficial. Both division and leaf cuttings are best done in the early stages of the growing period.

Watering indoors requires moderation

Since they thrive in low light, they are suitable for indoor window cultivation. During the growing period, water when the topsoil dries out, allowing water to flow out from the bottom of the pot. Be more conservative with watering during the semi-dormant period. Watering directly onto the leaves can cause leaf scorch, so water the soil instead. From left to right in the photo: 'Tamazusa', "Umbra Ticolara," *retusa* 'Yukihime', *obtusa*.

Dividing offsets

Haworthias grow rapidly and produce offsets at the base of the parent plant, forming clusters. Once a year, during the spring or fall growing seasons, let's divide the offsets while repotting. Below, we have repotted *turgida*.

BEFORE

AFTER

1

Gently loosen the root ball while being careful not to damage the thick, white, new roots. Discard the old roots along with the old soil.

2

Locate natural separation points of the offsets and detach them from the parent plant.

3

If offsets cannot be separated naturally, it's okay to gently snap them off. Even if the roots of the offsets are severed, they will sprout if left alone.

4

Remove any dead leaves from the base of the plant. They come off cleanly when pulled sideways.

5

On the left is the parent plant, and on the right are the two separated offsets. Plant them in separate pots.

6

Fill each pot with fresh potting soil and plant one offset in each. After planting, water generously until water flows out from the bottom of the pots.

Kalanchoe

BASIC DATA

Scientific name: **Kalanchoe**
Family: **Crassulaceae**
Genus: **Kalanchoe**
Also known as: **Ryukyu Benkei**
Native to: **Madagascar, South Africa, India, Malay Peninsula, China**
Growth type: **Summer type**
Propagation: **Division, stem cuttings, leaf cuttings**

The slender, elongated leaves covered with fine hairs resemble rabbit ears. In the West, some varieties fall under the common name of "panda plant" while in Japan the same varieties are in the "rabbit family." Most of these belong to the *tomentosa* species. Pictured left to right: 'Teddy Bear' with brown leaves, *nigromarginatas* with dark spots along the leaf margins, and 'Golden Girl' with yellow hairs appearing golden in the light.
* For varieties see pages 92–94
* Introduction of varieties on pages 92–94.

There are approximately 140 species of Kalanchoe, with around 120 species primarily distributed in Madagascar. They exhibit various characteristics such as hairy leaves, speckled patterns, velvety textures, dancing-like leaf shapes, and the production of small offsets along the leaf margins, resulting in a wide range of unique varieties. They vary in size from small plants about 4" (10cm) tall to shrubs reaching about 10' (3 meters). While they are easy to grow and thrive vigorously, they are particularly sensitive to cold, so it's important to ensure a sufficiently warm environment. Kalanchoe exhibits short-day photoperiodic flowering, meaning they bloom when daylight hours decrease.

Characteristics of Kalanchoe

Densely covered with fine hairs on the leaf surface

A type with the leaf surface covered in fine hairs. The species above is *nigromarginatas*. The fine hairs protect the leaves from intense sunlight but easily collect water. Direct exposure to sunlight can cause leaf scorch.

Numerous growth points along the leaf margins

Each serrated part of the leaf edge contains a growth point, from which new shoots emerge and cluster around the leaf, creating a humorous appearance. Eventually, these shoots grow into offsets. From left to right: *tubiflora* and *daigremontiana*.

Unique red-purple mottled patterns

These are characterized by thick, green leaves with red-purple mottled patterns. If the soil is too wet, the patterns may not develop well. For enjoying the leaves, it's recommended to keep the plants small. Pictured left to right: *humilis* and *marmorata*.

Some varieties turn red in fall

Some varieties exhibit fall foliage, with the leaves turning red as temperatures drop. Above is 'Fuyumomiji. As spring approaches and temperatures rise, the leaves gradually return to their original color. Since they flower from winter to spring, you can enjoy both the fall foliage and flowers.

Cultivation Calendar

	JAN	FEB	MAR	APR	MAY	JUN	JUL	AUG	SEP	OCT	NOV	DEC
Growth Period (Growing Season / Dormant Period)	Dormant period			Growing season							Slow growth period	
Flowering												
Transplanting, Dividing, Propagation by Cutting, Leaf Cuttings												
Fertilizer												

Daily Care

Watering and Fertilizing

During the growth period, water generously when the soil surface dries out. In summer, maintain slight drying. These plants are sensitive to cold and excessive water in winter weakens them, so reduce watering or mist every 2–3 weeks to maintain slight dryness and allow the plants to rest. Fertilize with slow-release fertilizer at the beginning of the growth period and provide diluted liquid fertilizer once a month.

Placement

During the growth period, place them outdoors in a sunny and well-ventilated area like a balcony. Avoid exposing them to prolonged rain during the rainy season. Strong summer sunlight can cause leaf scorch, so move them to a partially shaded location. These succulents are particularly susceptible to cold damage, so consider switching to indoor cultivation where the temperature remains above 41°F (5°C) in late November.

Transplanting and Pruning

Because the roots are thin and delicate, poor drainage can occur if the roots fill the pot, making them susceptible to root rot. It's advisable to repot them once a year, along with pruning if needed. For flowering varieties, pruning should be done after flowering. When repotting, gently loosen the root ball to improve compatibility with the new soil.

Propagation

You can propagate them through division, cuttings, or leaf cuttings, but cuttings are the most common method. Cut the stems into segments of about 2–3 nodes, remove the lower leaves, and let the cut ends dry in partial shade for about a week before inserting them into the soil. When managed in bright, indirect light, roots should develop in 3–4 weeks. You can also use removed leaves for leaf cuttings.

Continuous growth from growth points

Varieties like *Kalanchoe delagoensis* (left), *Kalanchoe hybrida* (center), and *Kalanchoe daigremontiana* (right) have growth points in each notch along the edges of their leaves. Unique baby plants emerge from the leaf tips and can be separated from the parent plant and placed in soil, where they will develop roots and grow.

Natural growth from fallen baby plants

Once the baby plants have grown to a certain size, they can easily detach from the parent, sometimes falling naturally onto the soil and growing on their own. These baby plants tend to grow vigorously during the summer but are susceptible to overwatering. Below you can see the pups of a 'Kodara Benkeiso'.

Propagation by Cuttings

This is done during the growth period from April to September (excluding the peak of summer in July and August). Using the cut stems during pruning ensures no waste.

Cut the stems into segments of about 2–3 nodes, and remove the lower leaves to make it easier to insert into the soil. Let the cut ends dry in partial shade for about one week to prevent stem bending over time.

Insert the cut end straight into new, dry potting soil.

Place 4 cuttings in one pot. When managed in a bright, well-ventilated, partially shaded area, they should develop roots in 3–4 weeks. Once roots have formed, begin watering.

Removed lower leaves can also be used for leaf cuttings

Prepare healthy lower leaves removed during propagation by cuttings simply by placing the, on dry soil. When managed in, well-ventilated, semi- shaded area, roots and shoots will gradually develop.

New shoots grow from where the stem was cut

Look closely at the base of the cut stem of *fedtschenkoi variegata* (left) used for cuttings, and you can see new shoots emerging from the leaf nodes. *Eriophylla* (right), covered in white fuzz, shows brown new shoots emerging from the center of the plant.

Euphorbia

BASIC DATA

Scientific name: **Euphorbia**
Family: **Euphorbiaceae**
Genus: **Euphorbia**
Native to: **Africa, Madagascar**
Growth type: **Summer type (some are winter types)**
Propagation: **Division, stem cuttings**

They form a large group distributed worldwide, with 500–1000 known species of succulents. They grow naturally in various regions and have evolved to adapt to their environments, resulting in diverse growth habits and forms. With characteristics resembling cacti, some have spines, grow columnar, spherical, or form clumps, offering endless allure. While there are both summer and winter types, this book focuses on the abundant summer varieties.

Characteristics of Euphorbia

Types with spines covering the entire body

Some species have so many spines that they are often mistaken for cacti. The photo shows *enopla*. Unlike cacti, which have white woolly parts called areoles at the base of the spines, Euphorbia's spines emerge directly from the stem.

White sap oozes from cuts

Cutting stems, leaves, or roots results in white sap oozing from the wound. This sap is toxic and can cause skin irritation, so be careful. When taking stem cuttings, rinse the cuttings thoroughly under running water and allow them to dry before planting. Pictured above is 'Kaimayoku'.

What appears to be flowers are actually "bracts"

The photo shows the "flowers" of *razafindratsirae*. The parts resembling yellow petals are actually modified leaves called "bracts." These bracts retain their color and shape for up to two months, while the actual flowers inside are tiny.

Euphorbias have a quirky appearance resembling cacti. From left to right in the photo: *razafindratsirae;* **'Variegata', which is pale and whitish due to lack of pigment; 'Obesablow';** *pulvinata;* **enopla, with striking red spines;** *anoplia;* **and 'Kaimagyoku', which has a pineapple-like shape.**
* Introduction of varieties on page 95.

Cultivation Calendar

	JAN	FEB	MAR	APR	MAY	JUN	JUL	AUG	SEP	OCT	NOV	DEC
Growth Period (Growing Season / Dormant Period)		Dormant period					Growing period					Dormant period
Flowering												
Transplanting, Dividing, Propagation by Cutting, Leaf Cuttings					Division, stem cuttings							
Fertilizer							Repotting					

*This book focuses only on summer types.

Daily Care

Watering and Fertilizing

Despite being summer types, they grow vigorously in both spring and fall, so water generously when the soil dries out during the growing period. They're sensitive to cold, so water sparingly during dormancy, but don't let them dry out completely. From late April to October, apply diluted liquid fertilizer about once a month.

Placement

Place them outdoors under a shelter where they can avoid rain but still receive sunlight and good airflow. Many species are sensitive to cold, so during winter, keep them indoors in a sunny location where the temperature is above 41°F (5°C).

Repotting and Pruning

Repotting should be done from late April to October when there is no risk of cold. Be careful, as cuts to leaves or spines may cause white sap to ooze, which can irritate the skin. Prune overcrowded branches or offsets during repotting if necessary.

Propagation

Propagate by stem cuttings or division from late April to June, using pruned branches or offsets. Rinse off the white sap from the cuts and let the cuttings dry in the shade for about a week before inserting into dry soil. You can also perform a stem cutting similar to cacti (see page 33).

Cactus

BASIC DATA

English name: **Cactus**

Family: **Cactaceae**

Genus: **Opuntia, Echinopsis, Selenicereus, etc., each with its own**

alias: **Cactus, Cactaceae, Haohoko**

Native to: **South America, North America, Central America**

Growth type: **Summer type**

Propagation: **Division, stem cuttings**

From the top left, *Cereus variabilis* f. *monstrosus* fro characterized by brown spines; *Echinocereus rigidissimus* var. *rubrispinus* with beautiful purple spines; representative species *Echinopsis calochlora* from the same genus. From the bottom left, *Espostoa lanata*, covered in white hairs; and *Opuntia debreczyi* with flat, fan-shaped stems.

* For varieties see pages 96–97

Cactus is a general term for plants belonging to the Cactaceae family, with over 2,000 species mainly found in the continents of North and South America. They have adapted to various climates and terrains, thriving in harsh environments such as desert regions and cool mountainous areas where other plants struggle to grow. Due to this adaptation, they have evolved independently, resulting in numerous genera with diverse characteristics. They are classified into categories such as columnar cacti, spherical cacti, and globular cacti based on the shape of their succulent stems. While many cacti have spines, some varieties lack them entirely.

Characteristics of Cacti

Presence of spines and areoles

The white woolly part at the base of the spines is called an areole, which is a modified, short, and degenerated branch. Some varieties lack spines. The transformation of leaf bases into spines is believed to help reduce water loss through transpiration. The photo shows *saglionis* from the Gymnocalycium genus.

Covered in white hairs

The white hairs covering the entire body are modified spines. The distinctive long hairs serve as sunshades to avoid direct sunlight and also function as protection against rain and moderate daily temperature fluctuations. The photo shows *melanostele* from the Espostoa genus.

Cultivation Calendar

	JAN	FEB	MAR	APR	MAY	JUN	JUL	AUG	SEP	OCT	NOV	DEC
Growth Period (Growing Season / Dormant Period)	Dormant period		Growing season				Semi-dormant period		Growing season			Dormant period
Flowering				Flowering								
Transplanting, Dividing, Propagation by Cutting, Leaf Cuttings				Division, stem cuttings					Repotting			
Fertilizer				Repotting					Repotting			

Daily Care

Watering and Fertilizing

During the growing season, water generously when the soil is dry. During the semi-dormant or slow growth period in summer, water sparingly, about once a week. During the dormant period in winter, withhold water completely or mist watering once a month. Use diluted liquid fertilizer about once a month in spring and fall.

Placement

From March to November, place them outdoors in a sunny and well-ventilated location whenever possible. Some species can survive outdoors during winter, but for added protection, place them in a makeshift frame to shield them from cold winds or manage them indoors in a sunny location.

Repotting and Pruning

Many cacti grow rapidly, so repot them into slightly larger pots once every 1–2 years during the first half of the growing season. It's easier to handle those with sharp spines with tweezers or thick gloves. If they become elongated or tall, you can perform a stem cutting* to reshape them.

Propagation

Species that produce offsets can be propagated by division. After division, let them dry for about 10 days in a well-ventilated, partly shaded area before planting. After planting, water them generously.

*About Stem Cutting
This involves cutting the main stem (trunk) of the plant. In this case, cut a relatively young portion of the stem, not the woody part near the base of the plant. For larger plants, using a sharp knife like a utility knife is recommended for a clean cut. New offsets will emerge and grow from the cut edge of the base. The cut upper portion of the stem should be allowed to dry thoroughly for 1–2 weeks before being inserted into dry soil.

Agave

BASIC DATA

Scientific Name: **Agave**
Family: **Asparagaceae**
Genus: **Agave**
Also known as: **Century Plant**
Origin: **Southern United States, Central and South America**
Growth Type: **Summer type**
Propagation: **Division, cuttings**

Starting from the upper left and moving clockwise, the fine thorns (serrations) along the edges of the leaves, reminiscent of dinosaur toes, in *pygmaea* 'Dragon Toes'; the narrow leaves spreading radially in *stricta*; the contrast between the dark blue-green leaves and the brown speckles bordering them in 'Blue Ember'; and the curling white filamentous fibers in *leopoldii*.

*For varieties see page 98

Agaves, cultivated in hot and dry soils, are popular for their wild appearance. The rosette-shaped leaves vary in shape and size, but all become more angular toward the tips, making their combination with thorns attractive. Some species can grow up to 13.1 ft (4 meters) in diameter. It takes over 10 years to bloom, and for some varieties, it takes so long that they are called "Century Flowers." After flowering, the plant dies.

Characteristics of Agave

Filamentous

Some types have white filamentous fibrous hairs on the edges of their leaves. These filamentous hairs are called "filaments." Pictured above is *leopoldii*.

Sharp thorns at the tip

Thorns come in various shapes and arrangements, creating beautiful sculptural beauty. Many varieties have sharp thorns at the tips of fleshy leaves. The photo is of *pygmaea* 'Dragon Toes'.

Cultivation Calendar

	JAN	FEB	MAR	APR	MAY	JUN	JUL	AUG	SEP	OCT	NOV	DEC
Growth Period (Growing Season / Dormant Period)	Dormant period		Growth period									Slow growth period
Flowering							●———————●					
Transplanting, Dividing, Propagation by Cutting, Leaf Cuttings			●———●						●———●			
Fertilizer				●———————●								

Daily Care

Watering and Fertilizing

During the growing season, water when the soil surface is dry. Avoid excess humidity in summer (July–August) and keep the plant somewhat dry to let it rest. During the dormant period in winter, water sparingly about once a month. In the early stages of the growing season (April–June), apply diluted liquid fertilizer once a month.

Placement

Since they prefer high temperatures and dry conditions, place them in a sunny spot with good ventilation to avoid rain. Many varieties are cold-resistant and can overwinter outdoors. However, they can be damaged by frost, so consider placing them in a makeshift frame or moving them indoors to protect them from severe cold.

Repotting

Repot in early spring or fall. Repotting every 2–3 years is recommended. For varieties with sharp thorns, it's advisable to wear thick gloves during the process.

Propagation

When offsets appear around the parent plant, divide them to propagate. It becomes difficult to produce offsets as the parent plant matures. You can divide them in early spring or fall, simultaneously with repotting. Remove as many roots as possible from the parent plant and plant them in another pot with dry soil. Start watering a week after planting.

Aloe

BASIC DATA

Scientific name: **Aloe**
Family: **Asphodelaceae**
Genus: **Aloe**
Also known as: **Rokai, Isha irazu (which means "doctor's not needed")**
Native to: **Africa, Madagascar, Arabian Peninsula**
Growth type: **Summer type**
Propagation: **Division, stem cuttings**

From the back left, we have the easily branching *ramosissima*, the striking *capitata* with red spines bordering powder blue leaves, and the *eximia* from Madagascar. From the front left, there's the spreading fan-like leaves of *suprafoliata*, the beautifully speckled 'Firebird', and *dicotomum*, a close relative of Aloe that grows over 8' (10 meters) tall in its native habitat. *For varieties see page 99

Medicinal varieties like Kidachi Aloe and edible types like Aloe vera have been cherished since ancient times, sturdy enough to be grown in gardens from Kanto to western Japan. Their flowers are also beautiful, with many species blooming in winter. There are over 500 species ranging from miniature ones about 2" (5cm) tall to treelike ones over 11 yd (10 meters) tall, each with its own unique characteristics like distinctive rosette forms or attractive leaf shapes and patterns. The group of large species that grow upright like Dicotoma is also known as Tree Aloes.

Characteristics of Aloe

Rosette and fan-shaped

Note the way the leaves unfold. There are types like *dicotoma*, which spread in a rosette form, and types like *suprafoliata*, which appear to have spread like a fan.

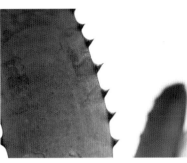

Spiny edges on leaves

There is a wide variety in how the spines grow. Some varieties have no spines, while others, like *capitata* in the picture, have densely spined leaf edges. Spine color and size also vary by variety, adding to their appeal.

Gel-like interior of leaves

Observe the cross-section of thick leaves. You can see they store moisture in a gel-like tissue.

Cultivation Calendar

	JAN	FEB	MAR	APR	MAY	JUN	JUL	AUG	SEP	OCT	NOV	DEC
Growth Period (Growing Season / Dormant Period)	Dormant period					Growing period						Slow growth period
Flowering	●											●
Transplanting, Dividing, Propagation by Cutting, Leaf Cuttings				●			●		●	●		
Fertilizer				●		●			●	●		

Daily Care

Watering and Fertilizing

During the growing season, water generously when the soil is dry. Be cautious of waterlogging from the rainy season to midsummer, and allow the soil to dry slightly. In winter, stop watering for varieties sensitive to cold, and for cold-resistant varieties, keep them slightly dry. Fertilize with diluted liquid fertilizer once a month in spring and fall.

Placement

Place in a sunny and well-ventilated spot throughout the year. Cold-resistant varieties can overwinter outdoors on balconies, but be cautious of freezing temperatures. For varieties not tolerant of cold, protect them from cold winds and frost by placing them in a simple frame or bringing them indoors.

Repotting and Pruning

Early spring and fall are ideal for repotting. Be careful of the spines during the process. Pruning to shape the plant can also be done at this time. You can let it grow naturally or prune to stimulate new growth. When repotting, remove damaged brown lower leaves. They come off cleanly when twisted sideways.

Propagation

If there are offsets around the parent plant, they can be divided during repotting to propagate. Alternatively, branches pruned during repotting in early spring and fall can be used for stem cuttings. Let the cuttings dry in partial shade for 1–2 weeks, then insert them into dry, fresh soil. Start watering after about a week.

Lithops

BASIC DATA

Scientific name: **Lithops**
Family: **Aizoaceae**
Genus: **Lithops**
Also known as: **Onnazen, Sekikaikiku**
Native to: **South Africa, Namibia**
Growth type: **Winter type**
Propagation: **Division**

From the top left, we have the *lesliei* var. *hornii* with a black-brown top surface; the 'Albinica' from the same family, and the *aucampiae*. From the middle row, there's the there's the *Lapidaria magaretae*, also called the Karoo Rose with patterns resembling a chrysanthemum emblem; the purple *julii* ssp. *fulleri* with crack patterns on its windowed part, the 'Fullergreen'. From the bottom left are the *bella,* the 'Top Red' with its distinctive red mesh pattern, and the *julii* ssp. *fulleri* with its crackle pattern.
*For varieties see page 100

Their natural habitat is the dry gravelly areas of South Africa. It's said that they evolved this unique form, where a pair of leaves and stems merged to mimic stones, to avoid being eaten by animals and adapt to their environment. They have transparent "windows" on their top surfaces with patterns, which are characteristic of absorbing light. They come in various colors and patterns like red, brown, green, and yellow, earning them the nickname "living jewels." Although there are about 40 basic species, there are many variations, attracting numerous collectors.

Characteristics of Lithops

Shedding skins in early spring

They undergo one shedding of skin annually for growth. When wrinkles appear on the leaves in spring, it's a sign of shedding. The old leaves split into two and peel away, revealing new leaves. Eventually, the old leaves shrink like skin, and new plants emerge.

Propagation by division

Although they appear flat like stones above ground, gently loosening the soil reveals their adorable elongated shapes below the surface. Remove damaged roots and shed skins from the base, then carefully separate the roots of both plants to make them equal.

Cultivation Calendar

	JAN	FEB	MAR	APR	MAY	JUN	JUL	AUG	SEP	OCT	NOV	DEC
Growth Period (Growing Season / Dormant Period)	Growing period	Slow growth period		Shedding		Dormant period				Growing period		
Flowering	⊷									⊶		
Transplanting, Dividing, Propagation by Cutting, Leaf Cuttings										⊶		
Fertilizer										⊶		

Daily Care

Watering and Fertilizing

From October to December, water generously when the soil surface is dry. From January to March, moisten the surface soil when it's dry. From April to May, keep the soil slightly dry when shedding begins. Overwatering may cause double shedding where new shoots also shed. From June to August, basically refrain from watering. Spraying the surface soil with a mist in the cool evening hours 2–3 times a month is beneficial. Apply diluted liquid fertilizer once a month from October to November.

Placement

Keep in a sunny, well-ventilated area under a roof that doesn't get direct rain. They're sensitive to waterlogqinq, so during summer, move to shaded areas or places that receive partial sunlight. Avoid places where the temperature drops below 41°F (5°C) in winter and keep them in a sunny indoor area with slightly dry conditions.

Repotting

Repot every 2–3 years, preferably in October or November. Gently remove the soil from the root ball, discard damaged roots and shed skins. Dry in shade for about a week, then plant in dry, well-draining soil with a small amount of slow-release fertilizer. Start watering gradually after a week.

Propagation

Divide plants in November, the same time as repotting. Similar to repotting, gently separate the roots after removing the soil and shed skins. Dry in shade for about a week, then plant in dry soil and start watering after a week.

Rhipsalis

BASIC DATA

Scientific name: **Rhipsalis**
Family: **Cactaceae**
Genus: **Rhipsalis**
Also known as: **Itoashi, Matsukaze**
Native to: **Central and South America**
Growth type: **Spring and fall type**
Propagation: **Division, stem cuttings**

Known as the forest cactus. From the top left, moving clockwise, we have the *kilbegeri* with its characteristic slender square stems, the cereus-like stems connected at each node of the *cereuscula*, the branching and drooping *capilliformis* with slender stems, the Hatiora's *salicornioides* species extending upward, and the densely branching *mesembryanthemoides*.
*For varieties see page 101

Although they are part of the cactus family, they lack spines and naturally grow as epiphytes on trees and rocks in tropical rainforests. Therefore, they prefer weak light and dislike direct sunlight. Bright shade is suitable for their growth. Their stems, which elongate like strings, have many nodes, and their free-spirited growth, bending and twisting, exudes a sense of dynamism. Trim excessive growth by cutting at the nodes. If you look closely at the tips of the stems, they branch out in a "scissors" shape, adding a charming touch to their appearance.

Characteristics of Rhipsalis

Naturally droop with weight

Stems with bamboo-like nodes tend to droop with growth. Planting them in hanging pots enhances their beauty. Pictured here is the *capilliformis*. When decorating near windows, rotate the pot gradually to ensure even growth, as the stems tend to stretch toward the sun.

Stylish variations

While slender stems are common, there are also stylish variants with broad, flat leaf-like stems, adding a fashionable touch. The photo shows the *elliptica*. New shoots are reddish-brown, creating a beautiful contrast with green.

Cultivation Calendar

	JAN	FEB	MAR	APR	MAY	JUN	JUL	AUG	SEP	OCT	NOV	DEC
Growth Period (Growing Season / Dormant Period)	Dormant period			Growing period			Slow growth period		Growing period		Slow growth period	
Flowering									●———●			
Transplanting, Dividing, Propagation by Cutting, Leaf Cuttings				●————————●					●————●			
Fertilizer				●————————●					●————●			

Daily Care

Watering and Fertilizing

During the growing period, water generously when the soil surface is dry. During the hot summer period, avoid overwatering to prevent root rot and manage them in a slightly dry state. In winter, water lightly about once every two weeks. If indoor dryness is a concern, spray with a mist. Apply diluted liquid fertilizer once a month from April to June and September to October.

Repotting and Pruning

Repot every 1–2 years. Avoid summer and winter and perform repotting in spring from April to June or fall from September to October. Trim excessive growth by cutting at any desired point above the nodes. Pruning can be done at any time throughout the year.

Placement

Since they inhabit shaded areas in the jungle, they prefer partial shade and dislike direct sunlight. Place them under a roof that avoids strong sunlight or indoors with partial shade. Ensure indoor management in winter to avoid temperatures below 41°F (5°C).

Propagation

Propagate by division and stem cutting. The ideal time is during repotting, avoiding extreme heat and cold. Branches pruned during repotting can be used for stem cuttings. Cut at a length of about 2¾–3⅛" (7–8cm) (cut above the nodes), dry the cut ends in shade for about two weeks, then insert them into dry, fresh soil. Start watering after 4–5 days.

Crassula

BASIC DATA

Scientific Name: **Crassula**

Family: **Crassulaceae**

Genus: **Crassula**

Native to: **South Africa, Madagascar, etc.**

Growth Type: **Spring-fall type**
(some are summer or winter types)

Propagation: **Division, stem cuttings**

Each with its own unique personality, characterized by differences in leaf expression and growth. From the top left, clockwise, when viewed from above, you'll see the green cross shape of the *perforata*; the captivating *fusca* with its blazing red foliage; the *conjuncta*, where leaves with red edges are stacked like towers; and the *radicans*, which blooms white flowers on red flower stalks in early spring.
*For varieties see pages 102–105

With an incredibly diverse range, there are said to be around 300 species of Crassula, primarily found in South Africa. They vary in size and growth habits, from small clumping forms to columnar, tower-like growth, and even shrub-like forms. The leaves also vary in shape and size, from rice grain-shaped to triangular and elliptical, providing a wealth of diversity. While there are spring-fall, summer, and winter types, the majority are spring-fall types. Many are small in size, with some varieties displaying beautiful fall foliage from fall to winter.

Characteristics of Crassula

Cross-shaped leaf stacking

When viewed from above, it's easy to see the triangular leaves beautifully stacked in a cross shape. One of the distinctive features is the alternate stacking of leaves to form a cross. Pictured here is *perforata*, also called "String of Buttons."

Columnar growth variations

Small leaves stack up, growing upward like a column. The thickness of the column varies depending on the variety. On the left you see the slim formations of the *lycopodioides* var. *pseudolycopodiodes*. The *muscosa*, on the right, has thicker, sturdier columns.

Cultivation Calendar

	JAN	FEB	MAR	APR	MAY	JUN	JUL	AUG	SEP	OCT	NOV	DEC
Growth Period (Growing Season / Dormant Period)	Dormant period			Growing season			Dormant period		Growing season			Slow growth period
Flowering												
Transplanting, Dividing, Propagation by Cutting, Leaf Cuttings												
Fertilizer												

* This book only covers information on spring-fall types.

Daily Care

Watering and Fertilizing

In spring and fall, water generously when the soil surface dries out. In summer (July–August), allow the soil to dry slightly before watering, about 4–5 days after the soil has dried out. In winter (January–February), water lightly when the leaves start to wrinkle. Fertilize with diluted liquid fertilizer once a month during the early stages of the growing season (March–May) and in September–October.

Placement

Place in a sunny and well-ventilated balcony or under eaves, avoiding prolonged rain during the rainy season. Provide partial shade during midsummer to prevent leaf scorching from strong sunlight. During the coldest periods, indoor cultivation is advisable.

Repotting and Pruning

Repot every 1–2 years, preferably at the beginning of the growing season. Repotting should coincide with growth to prevent root binding and ensure good drainage. Gently loosen the root ball, remove about a third of the soil, and replant in a slightly larger pot with fresh soil. Prune back overgrown or tangled stems. Repotting can be done simultaneously with pruning.

Propagation

Propagation can be done through division and stem cuttings. Use cut branches for stem cuttings. Allow the cut ends to dry in partial shade for about 1 week to 10 days, then insert them into dry soil. Divide clumps during repotting.

Aeonium

BASIC DATA

Scientific Name: **Aeonium**

Family: **Crassulaceae**

Genus: **Aeonium**

Native to: **Canary Islands, North Africa, etc.**

Growth Type: **Spring-fall type similar to winter type**

Propagation: **Division, stem cuttings**

Characterized by its glossy black leaves, the popular 'Zwartkop'; the refreshing green foliage of 'Lemonade'; the chic 'Velour' with its reddish-brown foliage; the rare flat rosette shape of *tabuliforme* var. *minima*; a solo 'Velour'; and the *rubrolineatum*, which catches the eye with its brown leaves and striped pattern.

* For varieties, see page **106**

Due to their natural habitat in regions with low rainfall, Aeoniums are resistant to drought but susceptible to overwatering. Many species grow upright, resembling shrubs, with rosette-shaped leaves resembling large flowers at the tips of their stems, making them visually appealing. With a variety of leaf colors, including black and variegated, their colors intensify when exposed to ample sunlight during the spring and fall growing seasons. Some Aeoniums may die after flowering, so it's advisable to cut off the flower stalks early to promote offsets.

Characteristics of Crassula

Beautiful rosette-shaped leaves

The leaves formed at the tips of the stems overlap densely, forming perfectly shaped rosettes reminiscent of flowers. The photo shows 'Velour' with rounded leaves.

Enjoy well-branched growth

As they grow, they become more erect, resembling shrubs. By pruning back elongated stems, new shoots and leaves emerge from below the cut, allowing you to shape the plant as desired. The photo shows 'Zwartkop'.

Cultivation Calendar

	JAN	FEB	MAR	APR	MAY	JUN	JUL	AUG	SEP	OCT	NOV	DEC
Growth Period (Growing Season / Dormant Period)	Dormant period		Growing season				Slow growth period	Dormant period		Growing season		
Flowering			●		●							
Transplanting, Dividing, Propagation by Cutting, Leaf Cuttings			●		●					●	●	
Fertilizer			●			●				●		●

Daily Care

Watering and Fertilizing

During the growing season, water generously when the soil surface dries out. Be cautious of overwatering during the summer and winter dormancy periods, as they are prone to root rot. Manage them by allowing the soil to dry slightly, watering about once or twice a month. Fertilize with diluted liquid fertilizer once a month during the growing season.

Repotting and Pruning

Repotting every 1–2 years is recommended, preferably at the beginning of the growing season. If you want to reduce elongation or reshape the plant, prune back during repotting to encourage new growth. Visualize the desired shape and prune accordingly to your preference.

Placement

Place them outdoors where they can receive ample sunlight and good air circulation. Avoid placing them where they'll receive direct rainfall during the rainy season, instead, place them under eaves for protection. During midsummer, keep them in a well-ventilated area with partial shade to avoid overheating. During winter, protect them from cold winds and frost by keeping them under eaves where temperatures stay above 41°F (5°C), or bring them indoors for wintering.

Propagation

Utilize cut stems from pruning for stem cuttings to propagate. Allow the cut ends to dry in partial shade for about 1 week, then insert them into dry, new potting soil. The ideal time for propagation is similar to repotting, during the early stages of the growing season. Divide clumps during repotting to propagate. Leaf cuttings are not suitable for propagation.

Cotyledon

BASIC DATA

Scientific Name: **Cotyledon**
Family: **Crassulaceae**
Genus: **Cotyledon**
Native to: **South Africa, southern Arabian Peninsula**
Growth Type: **Spring-fall type**
Propagation: **Division, stem cuttings**

There are varieties with distinctive features such as leaves resembling bear paws, those with eye-catching red borders, trailing small leaves, and silver-gray leaves with a powdery texture. Many species grow upright stems that eventually become woody and brown at the base. Some varieties extend long flower stems from early summer to fall, bearing bell-shaped flowers, adding to their charm. While they are tolerant of dry conditions, they dislike high temperatures and humidity, so avoid exposing them to prolonged rainfall.

Characteristics of Cotyledon

Fuzzy leaves

The fine hairs covering the surface of the leaves evolved to protect them from intense sunlight and dryness in their natural habitat. Leaves are prone to falling off in prolonged rain, so it's best to avoid excessive moisture. The photo shows *tomentosa* ssp. *ladismithensis* (one of the Bear's Paw varieties).

Powdery coating on leaves

The white powder covering the leaf surface serves the same purpose as the fuzz, protecting the leaves from strong light and dryness. Be cautious not to wet the leaves with rain or water as the powder easily washes off. The reddish edges of the leaves are also a characteristic feature of Cotyledon. The photo shows *undulata*.

From left to right, there are varieties with striking red borders like *orbiculate*; ones that spread out like a vine such as *pendens*; the *tomentosa ssp. ladismithensis*, commonly called "Bear's Paw," *undulata*, with large, frilled, silver-gray leaves; *elisae*, with charming bell-shaped flowers that bloom in early summer; and *ladismithensis* f. *variegata*, with cool white tones.

*For varieties see page 107

Cultivation Calendar

	JAN	FEB	MAR	APR	MAY	JUN	JUL	AUG	SEP	OCT	NOV	DEC
Growth Period (Growing Season / Dormant Period)	Dormant period		Growing season				Semi-dormant period		Growing season			Slow growth period
Flowering						Flowering						
Transplanting, Dividing, Propagation by Cutting, Leaf Cuttings												
Fertilizer												

Daily Care

Watering and Fertilizing

During the growing season, water generously when the topsoil is dry. For varieties with powdery leaves, water the soil directly to avoid wetting the leaves. They are susceptible to root rot, so reduce watering frequency in summer and allow the soil to dry slightly. During winter, water sparingly, around once or twice a month, to allow the plants to rest. Apply diluted liquid fertilizer monthly during the early growth stages in March–May and September–October.

Placement

During the growing season, place them in a sunny and well-ventilated balcony or under an eave. In hot and humid summers, move them to partial shade to avoid intense sunlight. During winter, protect them from cold winds and frost and place them indoors near a sunny window where the temperature does not drop below 41°F (5°C).

Repotting and Pruning

Repotting should be done every 1–2 years during the early growth stages of the growing season. Use slow-release fertilizer as a base and transplant into a slightly larger pot. If you wish to rejuvenate elongated plants or reshape their form, prune them during repotting.

Propagation

They can be propagated through division or stem cuttings. If the base of the plant has multiple stems clustered together, division is possible. For stem cuttings, use healthy and sturdy branches pruned during maintenance. Allow the cut ends to dry in partial shade for about 1 week to 10 days, then plant them in dry soil. Start watering after about a week.

Graptopetalum
and Graptosedum

Various Rosette Types. Starting from the top left and going clockwise, we have *mendozae*, which forms a cluster of pink to reddish small leaves; 'Francesco Baldi', with overlapping elongated leaves; 'Bronze', known for its impressive bronze color; and *paraguayense,* displaying beautiful shades of gray. *Mendozae* and *paraguayense* belong to the Graptopetalum genus, while the remaining two are Graptosedum species. *For varieties see page 108

BASIC DATA

Scientific Name: **Graptopetalum, Graptosedum**
Family: **Crassulaceae**
Genera: **Graptopetalum, Graptosedum**
Native Range: **Southwestern United States to Mexico**
Growth Type: **Spring-Fall type**
Propagation: **Division, stem cuttings, leaf cuttings**

Graptopetalum is known for its rosette-shaped, fleshy leaves that resemble flowers when fully opened. It belongs to a group similar to Echeveria (page 18), with upright stems and many species that exhibit beautiful reddish foliage. It often produces offsets at the base, eventually forming clusters. In the spring to summer, it also blooms with yellow or orange flowers.

Graptosedum is a hybrid of Graptopetalum and Sedum (page 14). Another hybrid is Graptobelia, which results from crossing Graptopetalum with Echeveria (page 18).

Characteristics of Graptopetalum and Graptosedum

Stems easily become leggy

When they grow, the stems elongate and stand upright. Placing them in a location with insufficient sunlight can result in elongated growth, so make sure to expose them to adequate sunlight to maintain a compact form. The photo shows the fast-growing *Graptopetalum paraguayense* (Ghost plant).

They can be easily propagated through leaf cuttings

Many varieties, such as *Graptopetalum bartramii* (Bartrum's stonecrop) and *Graptopetalum mendozae* are known for their characteristic of leaves easily falling off with just a touch. Varieties with easily detachable leaves tend to produce shoots readily when propagated from leaf cuttings, making the orientation of the leaf cuttings important.

Cultivation Calendar

	JAN	FEB	MAR	APR	MAY	JUN	JUL	AUG	SEP	OCT	NOV	DEC
Growth Period (Growing Season / Dormant Period)	Slow growth period	Dormant period		Growing season				Semi-dormant period		Growing season		
Flowering				Flowering								
Transplanting, Dividing, Propagation by Cutting, Leaf Cuttings			●						●	●		
Fertilizer			●		●				●	●		

Daily Care

Watering and Fertilizing

When the surface of the soil is dry, water generously. In summer, water sparingly to allow it to dry out slightly. In winter, almost no watering is needed. For indoor cultivation, mist the leaves once or twice a month. Fertilize with a diluted liquid fertilizer once a month during the early growth period from March to May and in mid-September to October. Be cautious about over-fertilizing as it can lead to elongation and difficulty in achieving vibrant leaf colors.

Placement

Maintain your plant in a well-lit and well-ventilated location on a sunny balcony or under eaves. In indoor or shaded conditions, the plant tends to elongate, so be sure to provide adequate sun.

Repotting and Pruning

Hardy varieties like *Graptopetalum paraguayense* and *Graptopetalum bartramii* withstand frost and freezing temperatures if protected. Repot in the early stages of the growth period. If the roots are crowded, gently remove a third of the old soil from the root ball and transplant it into a slightly larger pot. Handle the leaves as little as possible, as they are prone to falling off. If the plant has grown too tall, you can trim it during repotting.

Propagation

You can propagate through division, stem cuttings, and leaf cuttings. When repotting, you can place the removed leaves on top of soil in partial shade, and new shoots will emerge. For stem cuttings, let the cut ends dry in partial shade for about 7-10 days, and then insert them into dry potting soil. Begin watering after one week.

Pachyphytum and Pachyveria

Scientific Name: **Pachyphytum • Pachyveria**
Family: **Crassulaceae**
Genera: **Pachyphytum genus, Pachyveria genus**
Native Range: **Mexico**
Growth Type: **Spring-Fall Type**
Propagation: **Division, stem cuttings, leaf cuttings**

From the upper left: 'Tsukibijin' with its pale purple-tinted leaf tips, and *hialium* with its sharp, pointed leaf tips. In the center is *compactum* with its uniquely sculpted leaves. From the lower left: 'Gekkabijin' with its glamorous presence, and 'Blue Mist' with its chic reddish-purple color. 'Blue Mist' and *hialium* are Pachyveria, while the other three are Pachyphytum.
*For varieties see page 109

With plump and fleshy leaves that resemble a delicate dusting of white powder, they have a beautiful and popular appearance. Some varieties grow with upright stems, creating a dynamic presence. If their shape becomes irregular, feel free to cut and reshape them to keep them compact. Insufficient sunlight can lead to poor leaf color and elongation, so ensure they receive ample sunlight during their growth period. Pachyveria is a hybrid variety of Pachyphytum and Echeveria (page 18), and they look quite similar.

Features of Pachyphytum · Pachyveria:

Plump leaves

Their plump, round, leaves have a lot of charm. Leaf size and shape may vary depending on the variety, making for a lot of fun diversity. The photo shows the polyhedral leaves of *Pachyphytum compactum,* which look like they've been carved to create facets.

Types with a white powdery coating

Although leaf colors may differ, many varieties have leaves covered with a white powdery coating. The photo features *Pachyphytum oviferum 'Tsukibikjin'.* Be careful not to expose them to rain or touch them since contact removes the powder on the leaf surface.

Cultivation Calendar

	JAN	FEB	MAR	APR	MAY	JUN	JUL	AUG	SEP	OCT	NOV	DEC
Growth Period (Growing Season / Dormant Period)	Dormant period				Growing season			Semi-dormant period		Growing season		Slow growth period
Flowering												
Transplanting, Dividing, Propagation by Cutting, Leaf Cuttings												
Fertilizer												

Daily Care

Watering and Fertilizing

Since their plump leaves store a lot of moisture, it's best to allow them to dry out slightly. During the growth period, water generously when the topsoil has dried out, usually 2–3 days later. In summer, water every 10 days in the evening when it cools down. In winter, maintain slightly dry conditions. When the leaves wrinkle, give a little water. Go easy on fertilizer to prevent excessive elongation. Use diluted liquid fertilizer during the early stages of growth.

Placement

During the growth period, place them in a well-ventilated area with ample sunlight. It's advisable to keep them under eaves to protect the white powder on their leaves from getting washed away by rain. In midsummer, avoid direct sunlight and place them in partial shade. In winter, protect them from cold and move them to a sunny indoor location.

Transplanting and Pruning

Transplanting is best done during the early stages of the growth period, approximately once every 1–2 years into a slightly larger pot. Be careful not to rub off the white powder on the leaf surface while transplanting, and handle them gently. When cutting back plants that are not too noticeable, it's good to trim the lower part during transplanting to maintain their shape.

Propagation

They can be propagated through division, cuttings, or leaf cuttings. Leaves that easily come off can be used for leaf cuttings. Place leaves on top of soil in partial shade to encourage sprouting. For cuttings, use pruned stems. Allow the cut stem ends to dry well in partial shade for about 1–10 days, then insert them into dry soil. Start watering one week later.

Sempervivum

BASIC DATA

Scientific Name: **Sempervivum**
Family: **Crassulaceae**
Genus: **Sempervivum**
Also known as: **Houseleek**
Native to: **High mountain areas of central and southern Europe**
Growth Type: **Spring-fall type**
Propagation: **Division, stem cuttings**

Clockwise from the top left, we have the deep tones of 'Black Mini', the gossamer look of arachnoideum 'Cobweb Joy' and 'Gazelle', 'the crisp intense greens of 'Sprite', 'Sakai', and 'More Honey', and the varying degrees of purple in 'Bronco', *tectorum* 'Red Purple', and 'Aldo Moro'
*For varieties see page 110.

Popular in Europe for a long time, Sempervivum comes in various sizes and richly colored rosette-shaped leaves. Some types even resemble wrapped white threads, exuding delicate and bold beauty. They are resilient to dryness and cold, and the changing leaf colors during the fall season and early spring are also delightful. From mature and thriving plants, runners extend with offsets, forming clusters of new plants. While they produce flower stems from the center of the rosettes, flowering signals the end of that particular plant's life cycle.

Features of Sempervivum

Propagation via offsets

When the pot is full of offsets, gently remove them with roots attached. Remove any dead leaves and plant them in another pot. Ease of division and propagation is one of their appealing traits.

Propagation via runners

In spring, runners emerge from the base of rosette-shaped leaves and produce offsets. Once the offsets on the runners reach a certain size, cut them from the tip of the runner and plant them.

Cultivation Calendar

	JAN	FEB	MAR	APR	MAY	JUN	JUL	AUG	SEP	OCT	NOV	DEC
Growth Period (Growing Season / Dormant Period)	Slow growth period			Growing season				Semi-dormant period		Growing season		Slow growth period
Flowering												
Transplanting, Dividing, Propagation by Cutting, Leaf Cuttings												
Fertilizer												

Daily Care

Watering and Fertilizing

During the growing season, water generously when the soil surface is dry. They are drought-tolerant, so be cautious not to overwater. Be mindful of heat and humidity, allowing the soil to dry slightly during summer. Similar management applies during winter. Apply diluted liquid fertilizer monthly during the early growth stages in spring and fall.

Placement

They are cold-resistant and can even overwinter outdoors during winter. They dislike hot and humid conditions in summer, so place them in a well-ventilated, partial shade area to keep them cool during summer. During spring and fall, manage them in areas with good sunlight exposure, ventilation, and rain protection.

Repotting

Spring (March–May) and fall (mid-September to October) are suitable times for repotting. Repotting every 1–2 years is recommended as they have a well-developed root system. Use well-draining soil to prevent root rot, especially during hot and humid periods.

Propagation

During repotting, varieties suitable for division can be separated or propagated through stem cuttings. Divide offsets growing in clusters and turn them into new plants. Cut off the tips of runners carrying offsets and use them for stem cuttings. Allow all offsets to dry in partial shade for about a week before planting. Begin watering them one week after planting.

Senecio and Othonna

BASIC DATA

Scientific Name: **Senecio, Othonna**

Family: **Asteraceae**

Genus: **Senecio, Othonna**

Native to: **Africa, Madagascar, India, Mexico**

Growth Type: **Spring-fall type, summer type, winter type (varies by species)**

Propagation: **Division, stem cuttings**

Clockwise from the left, we have *scaposus* wrapped in white fibers, followed by *haworthii* with almond-like leaves, *kleiniformis*, with its claw-like leaf tips, 'Masai no Yajiri' named after its leaf shape, *capensis* 'Ruby Necklace' with impressive purple stems, and 'Peach Necklace' with leaves resembling peaches. In the far back we see the tips of *herreanus*. 'Ruby Necklace' is an Othonna, while all others are Senecio.
*For varieties see page 111.

Senecio and Othonna, members of the Asteraceae family. Originating from dry regions, they dislike high humidity, but due to their fine roots, they are also sensitive to extreme dryness. Be careful not to let them dry out too much. Senecio offers a variety of cultivars, including trailing types and those covered in white hairs. Senecio has three growth types depending on the cultivar, while all Othonna varieties go dormant in summer, showing a dislike for summer heat.

Features of Senecio • Othonna

Beautiful silver leaves

Leaves covered in delicate white hairs are soft and have a velvety texture, creating a beautiful appearance. Continuous exposure to rain may cause the hairs to shed, so be cautious during prolonged rainy periods or when watering. The photo shows *Senecio haworthii*).

Trailing succulent leaves

The plump, fleshy leaves grow along slender trailing stems, creating a cascading effect. Placing them on the edge of a pot allows them to trail gracefully. Pictured here is *Senecio* 'Peach Necklace'.

Cultivation Calendar

	JAN	FEB	MAR	APR	MAY	JUN	JUL	AUG	SEP	OCT	NOV	DEC
Growth Period (Growing Season / Dormant Period)	Dormant period		Growing season					Semi-dormant period		Growing season		Slow growth period
Flowering												
Transplanting, Dividing, Propagation by Cutting, Leaf Cuttings												
Fertilizer			Spring-fall type, summer type					Spring-fall type, winter type				

Daily Care

Watering and Fertilizing

Avoid overwatering as they are prone to root rot in high humidity. Water only when the soil has dried out. During the growing season, water generously. In midsummer and midwinter, maintain a slightly dry condition without completely withholding water to prevent root drying. Apply diluted liquid fertilizer monthly during the early growth stages in spring and fall for spring-fall types, and in spring for summer types, and in fall for winter types.

Repotting and Pruning

Repot every 1–2 years during the early growth stages of the growing season. Prepare a pot one size larger, gently loosen the root ball, remove about ⅓ of the soil, and replant in fresh soil. Trim off dead leaves and consider pruning during repotting.

Placement

During the growing season, place them in a sunny and well-ventilated area like a balcony or under an eave, but be cautious of rain. Direct sunlight in summer can cause leaf scorch and weaken the plant, so place them in bright partial shade. In winter, protect them by placing them in a makeshift frame or indoors in a bright location.

Propagation

During repotting, use cut stems for stem cuttings to propagate. Trim stems to about 1–2" (4–5cm) in length. Allow the cut ends to dry in partial shade for about 1–2 weeks, then plant them in dry soil. Begin watering after about a week. Division can also be done during this time.

Things to Know for Long and Healthy Growth

Many succulent plants grow quickly, so if grown over a long period, their shape can become distorted or their roots can become too dense. To maintain their shape and health, it's good to occasionally prune and repot them.

Repotting

Repotting every 1–2 years is fundamental. This process helps to remove old roots, allowing new roots to grow. If you neglect repotting for an extended period soil can become compacted, reducing air circulation and potentially leading to root rot. The photo shows an *Echeveria* 'Elianodo' that has been in the pot for about two years, with dried and crispy lower leaves.

BEFORE   AFTER

1. Gently remove the dried lower leaves by hand. Place a mesh over the pot's drainage hole and fill the bottom of the pot with about ⅕ of gravel.

2. Spread a thin layer of succulent potting mix over the gravel.

3. Add a small amount of slow-release fertilizer as a base fertilizer. Cover it with more potting mix until the fertilizer is concealed

4. Carefully remove the plant from its pot, shake off the old soil, and trim the old roots to tidy up the root ball.

5. Place the plant on top of the pot and support it with one hand. Using a small trowel, slowly fill in the gaps with potting mix, ensuring that no soil gets onto the leaves.

6. Once filled with potting mix, gently tap the pot with a trowel to settle the soil between the roots and stabilize the plant. Then, water generously.

Pruning Overgrown Plants

Succulents that grow tall and become bushy need pruning to maintain their shape. If the lower leaves are lost, it can leave the plant looking bare, so trimming them back is essential. The photo shows an overgrown *Sedum adolphi* whose shape has become distorted. The cuttings can be used for propagation by planting them in pots, and new shoots will emerge from the pruned stem base, allowing the plant to regenerate.

BEFORE   AFTER

1 Cut back the elongated stems from the base of the plant, being careful not to damage any emerging new shoots.

2 Cut the shorter branches, leaving 2–3 leaves at the bottom. New shoots will emerge from the remaining leaf nodes.

3 Cut the tip of the branches at a length of ⅞–1⅛" (2–3cm).

4 Repeat the process for all the branch tips. The tips can be used for stem cuttings, while the remaining leaves on the branches can be used for leaf propagation. Allow the cuttings to dry in the shade for about a week.

5 Fill a new pot with potting mix and insert the cuttings from step 4. Remove the lower leaves for easier insertion. The removed leaves can be used for leaf propagation. The "After" photo shows the appearance of the pot after two months.

6 Two months after pruning the elongated stems in step 2, new shoots are beginning to emerge from the base of the parent plant.

Various Methods of Propagation

As detailed on each variety's page, there are primarily three methods of propagation: stem cuttings, leaf cuttings, and division. The method of propagation varies depending on the type of growth, so refer to the variety pages in PART 1 to experience the joy of propagation.

Stem Cuttings

Plants with elongated stems that grow upright can be propagated by cutting the tip and inserting it into the soil. This method is called stem cutting. Succulents root best when they are dry, so it's crucial to let the cuttings dry before inserting them into dry potting soil. When making the cut, leaving 4–5 leaves at the base promotes the emergence of new shoots from the original plant. Use healthy stems whenever possible.

Remove the lower leaves to make it easier to insert into the soil. Let the cuttings dry in the shade for 1–2 weeks before inserting them into dry potting mix. The removed leaves can be used for leaf propagation. Water the cuttings approximately one week after insertion, once roots have formed. Pictured here is *Sedum 'Golden Glow'*.

Leaf Propagation

Many succulents easily drop their leaves which, when detached from the stem, do not wither but produce new shoots from the growth point. Leaf propagation utilizes this characteristic. Varieties that are easy to detach by touch are more suitable for leaf propagation. If the leaves are challenging to remove, a different propagation method may be more suitable. Leaf propagation is simple—just place the leaves on dry soil. It's really gratifying to watch them grow.

Place new potting mix in a shallow container and lay the leaves on top. Small leaves will sprout from the base (growth point) of the leaf and eventually grow into new plants. Once roots have formed, start watering and keep the container in a bright, airy location with partial shade. The new plants will grow by absorbing nutrients from the original large leaf, causing the original leaf to gradually wither. Pictured here is a Sedum variety.

Division

Plants that spread horizontally may become root-bound in their pots if the roots grow too much, causing poor water absorption. Divide the plants, loosen the roots, and replant them in smaller sections. Similarly, for varieties that produce offsets and grow into clusters, dividing the offsets and planting them separately in pots will promote healthy growth for each individual plant.

Remove the root ball from the pot, use your fingers to find the natural root divisions, and start separating the roots. Untangle the intertwined stems and leaves with your thumb, and similarly divide the above-ground parts. You can trim the lower part of the roots to fit the size of the pot. The photo shows *Sedum* Little Missy' (also called *Crassula* 'Petit Bicolor')

PART 2

Arranging
Succulents

Combining Single Pots

A "single pot" where only one type of plant is planted is easy to care for and easy to grow because it can be tailored to the characteristics of each plant. Furthermore, since you can easily move it from place to place, you can enjoy it in a variety of settings.

Outdoors

Arranging under the eaves

Arranging pots of the same material next to each other creates a sense of unity throughout the shelf. Varying the sizes and heights of the pots adds a sense of style to the display. The left photo shows, from the top left: 'Kurotoji', *rogersii*, 'Velour', *orgyalis*, 'Tom Thumb', *burrito,* and from the bottom left: *scapigera,* 'Aurora', *alternum, cordeta.*

If you want to make the most of limited space, shelves where you can display plants vertically are convenient. Simply arranging small pots with individual personalities such as Sedum with dynamic growth upward or spreading horizontally, Kalanchoe with interesting textures like fluffiness or velvety appearance, and Crassula with enjoyable leaf colors and shapes can create a cute display. Rearranging them according to your mood makes it easy to change the corner's appearance.

'Aurora', *alternum*, and *burrito* are Sedum; 'Kurotoji, *orgyalis*, and *scapigera* Kalanchoe; 'Tom Thumb', *rogersii*, and *cordeta* are Crassula. 'Velour' is Aeonium.

Hanging from trees

Hanging your plants allows air to circulate, helping the moisture in the pots dry out more easily,—especially beneficial for plants that dislike excessive humidity. From left in the photo: 'Ruby Necklace', *capilliformis*, and *rowleyanus*.

Shady areas under trees that soften the strong summer sunlight are cool, bright, and well-ventilated, making them perfect spots for succulents. We hung trailing succulents like Rhipsalis, which have beautiful cascading forms, at varying heights. Balancing pots of different sizes also enhances the overall aesthetic. On rainy days or in winter, move them under the eaves or to a bright indoor location above 41°F (5°C).

---

* 'Ruby Necklace' is Othonna, *capilliformis* is Rhipsalis, *rowleyanus* is Senecio.

Displaying on shelves

Haworthia, which does not like direct sunlight, can be enjoyed as indoor greenery. It's satisfying to create a dedicated display shelf in a bright room. Similarly, the Rhipsalis, which prefers low light, is arranged at the bottom left to add some variety. The cactus in the upper left can also be grown indoors if managed with less watering. Since light comes from only one direction, rotate the pots occasionally to ensure even exposure.

The middle section becomes the focal point of the shelf. Planting in matching pots gives rhythm to the display, enhancing the individual characteristics of each variety. In the photo above, from the left on the upper row: *Epostoa melanostele*, *Echinopsis eyriesii*, from the left on the middle row: 'Mirror Ball', *picta*, and *pilfera*, and from the left on the lower row: *kirbergii*, *obutusa*, and *cuspidata*.

* *Epostoa melanostele* and *Echinopsis eyriesii* are cacti, *kirbergii* is Rhipsalis, and all others are Haworthia.

Placing by the window

If you want to grow striking Agaves, Aloes, and Cacti indoors with their beautiful sharp thorns and wild appearance, choose a bright window where they can receive plenty of sunlight. To enhance the charm of succulents, all the pots are in a calm antique-style tin. Since indoor areas have poorer ventilation than outdoors, watering should be moderate, allowing the soil to dry out slightly.

Agave, Aloe, and Cacti are all summer types that dislike the cold. Grouping plants with similar characteristics makes them easier to manage. From left to right: *eximia, isismensis, capitata*, and *Astrophytum ornatum*.

* *Isismensis* is Agave, *Astrophytum ornatum* is Cactus, and all others are Aloe.

Arranging in Clusters

Combining succulent plants to create an "arranged planting" brings out new charm as they complement each other. Knowing the characteristics and growth habits of each plant before combining them ensures easier care and enjoyment throughout the growing process.

Using Only Sedum

With their small and adorable leaves, as well as a wide variety of species, Sedums are popular succulents. Since they tend to grow horizontally and extend their branches, choosing a tall container and planting them to hang over the edge creates a natural atmosphere. When using two or more species, planting different varieties next to each other and intertwining their branches haphazardly is the key to creating a delightful display.

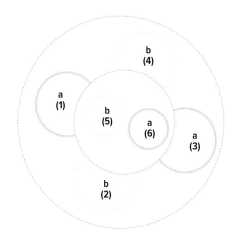

b
(4)

a
(1)

b
(5)

a
(6)

a
(3)

b
(2)

Succulents Used:
a: Sedum oryzifolium f. albiflora (p.83)
b: Sedum makinoi f. variegata (p.84)

Materials needed:
For the upper layer: a tin container with a diameter of 3⅛" (8cm) and a height of 2¾" (7cm)
For the lower layer: a tin container with a diameter of 6" (15cm) and a height of 4¾" (12cm)
* Use a compost-shaped container (lower layer) and stack a cup-shaped container with the same texture on top.
* Make drainage holes at the bottom (➜ p.80).

1

Separate the *oryzifolium f. albiflora* and *makinoi f. variegata* from a single potted seedling in a ratio of 2:2:1.

2

You will plant both varieties divided in a 2:2 ratio in the lower tier. To prepare, loosen and spread the roots horizontally for each divided plant and make sure the seedlings lie flat.

3

Spread the *oryzifolium f. albiflora* horizontally in the lower tier (1). Plant the *makinoi f. variegata* in the same way (2), intertwining it with the *oryzifolium f. albiflora*.

4

Repeat step 3 on the other side of the lower tier, (3, 4). In the upper tier, spread the remaining divided plants (step 1), planting them to blend with each other (5, 6).

TIP: To maintain balance, it's important to trim Sedums before they grow and cover the pot completely, keeping their shape intact.

Combining Rosette-Type Varieties

Creating a succulent arrangement by combining different succulent plants allows each plant to enhance the beauty of the others, resulting in a unique charm. By understanding the characteristics and growth patterns of each succulent before combining them, you can maintain them easily and enjoy the growth process.

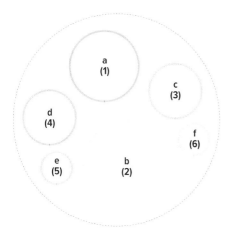

Succulents Used:
a: Echeveria 'Laurinze' (p.89)
b: Graptopetalum 'Purple King' (p.108)
c: Echeveria 'Domingo' (p.88)
d: Echeveria 'Ilia' (p.86)
e: Echeveria *elegans* 'Alba' (p.86)
f: Echeveria 'Nobaranosei' (p.88)

Materials needed:
Colander with a diameter of 8½" (22cm) and a height of 4¼" (11cm) (excluding handles)

1. Plant 'Laurinze' (1), and then plant 'Purple King' (2). When you have larger plants, it's easier to achieve balance by planting the larger ones first.

2. Plant 'Domingo' (3), and on the opposite side, plant 'Ilia' (4). In the foreground, plant the mini-sized 'Alba' (5). Finally, plant 'Nobaranosei', and your arrangement is complete (6).

TIP: To match the color of the colander we used as a pot, we unified the arrangement with varieties that have a silvery, pale hue.

Combining the "Rabbit-eared" Kalanchoe

With oval leaves covered in white fuzz and resembling rabbit ears, Kalanchoe plants from the same family exhibit individual differences in color and speckling, which are distinguishing characteristics among varieties. What they share is a mature, grayish vibe. When paired with charming pots, they exude tranquility.

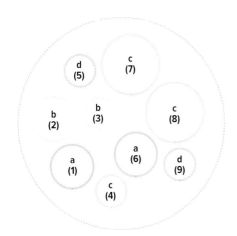

Succulents Used:
a: Kalanchoe 'Golden Girl' (p.92)
b: Kalanchoe eriophylla (p.92)
c: Kalanchoe tomentosa (p.92)
d: Kalanchoe tomentosa f. nigromarginatas (p.92)

Materials needed:
Tin container with a diameter of 4¼" (11cm) and a height of 2¾" (7cm)
Make drainage holes in the bottom (refer to p.80).
Small pebbles of Akadama soil
Decorative picks

Plant 'Golden Girl' slightly away from the edge of the container (1). Creating gaps between the edge of the container and the succulents enhances the fluffy texture.

Behind 'Golden Girl' plant both large and small seedlings of *eriophylla* (2, 3). Plant the smaller ones toward the center. Plant *tomentosa* in front of 'Golden Girl' to the right (4).

Plant *tomentosa* f. *nigromarginatas* followed by 'Golden Girl' (5, 6), then plant *tomentosa* at the back (7).

Complete by planting *tomentosa* followed by *tomentosa* f. *nigromarginatas* (8, 9). Planting shorter seedlings in the foreground ensures that all varieties are visible from the front.

Finish by lightly spreading Akadama soil across the surface. This enhances the dry texture characteristic of the fluffy appearance. Finally, insert decorative picks to complete the arrangement.

TIP: The *tomentosa* species, with its white fuzz and brown spots, has many variants, such as 'Star', 'Teddy Bear' (page 92), and others.

Using Trailing Types

Compact and trailing succulents, with their creeping growth habit, look charming when planted to spill over the edge of a pot. Using slightly mature seedlings enhances the natural impression. Instead of planting just one type, incorporating different varieties with similar characteristics creates the illusion of a single plant, offering delicate expressions.

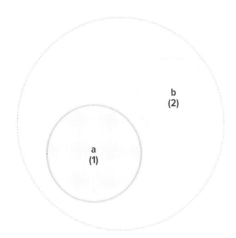

Succulents Used:
a: Graptosedum "Little Gem" (p.108)
b: Crassula remota (p.105)

Materials needed:
Unglazed ceramic pot with a diameter of 4¾" (12cm) and a height of 3¾" (9.5cm)

Using both hands, spread 'Little Gem' out flat. Plant it so that it spills out over the edge of the pot (1). Envisage it blending into the *remota* that will be planted next.

Plant *remota* in the remaining space, leaving no gaps between the two plants (2).

TIP: This planting method is suitable for varieties with similar shapes and sizes, allowing for easy gradation of colors.

Using Vertical Types

Succulents that grow upward contribute to creating a beautiful silhouette and are ideal for creating arrangements with varying heights. When planting, it's fundamental to position them toward the back as the core of the arrangement. Their strong vertical lines emphasize a glamorous impression. Beginners may find it easier to select varieties with similar leaf shapes.

Left

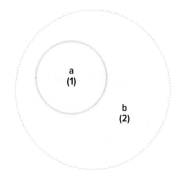

a
(1)

b
(2)

Succulents Used:
a: Sedum adophi 'Golden Glow' (p.82)
b: Crassula rogersii (p.105)

Materials needed:
Porcelain cup with a diameter of 3⅜" (8.5cm)
and a height of 3⅛" (8cm)
* As the base has no drainage holes, add a medium
to prevent root rot (➜p.80).
Large-sized pumice as pot bottom stones

Plant 'Golden Glow' (1), then plant the shorter *rogersii* to
its right (2). It's easier to plant taller varieties first. Finally,
spread pumice on the soil surface to finish.

TIP: The leaves of the *Kalanchoe orgyalis* differ in
color on the top and underside. Kalanchoe brachteata
and Kalanchoe millotii were chosen to match the gray
tones of the leaves' underside.

Right

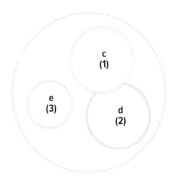

c
(1)

e
(3)

d
(2)

Succulents Used:
c: Kalanchoe orgyalis (p.93)
d: Kalanchoe bracteata (p.93)
e: Kalanchoe millotii (p.94)

Materials needed:
Porcelain bowl with a diameter of 6" (15cm) and
a height of 3" (7.5cm)
* As the base has no drainage holes, add a medium
to prevent root rot (➜p.80).
Large-sized pumice as pot bottom stones

Plant *orgyalis* which serves as the core, toward the back (1).
Plant *brachteata,* which is of medium height, to its right (2).

Plant the shorter *millotii* toward the front (3). Finally, spread
pumice on the soil surface to finish.

There's something quirky and solid about compact, clumping succulents that propagate offspring around the parent plant. Arrangements that utilize their irregular shapes look kind of like puzzles. Leaving space between plants enhances each plant's outline, and brings unique character to the composition. The angle at which they're planted affects the overall mood.

Top

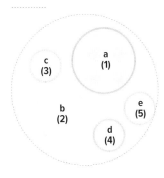

Succulents Used:
a: Pachyveria 'Blue Mist' (p.109)
b: Graptobryum 'A Grim One' (p.108)
c: Echeveria elegans (p.87)
d: Graptopetalum mendozae (p.108)
e: Sedeveria 'Yellow Humbert' (p.85)

Materials needed:
Pottery with a diameter of 6" (15cm) and a height of 2⅜" (6cm)
* As the base has no drainage holes, add a medium to prevent root rot (➡p.80).

Plant the eye-catching 'Blue Mist' slightly toward the back on the right, and 'A Grim One' toward the front left (1, 2). Continue, planting *elegans*, *mendozae*, and 'Yellow Humbert' in that order (3–5).

Middle

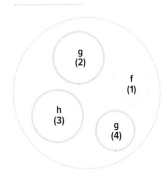

Succulents Used:
f: Pachyphytum 'Momobijin' (p.109)
g: Sinocrassula densirosulata (p.105)
h: Sedum morganianum (p.83)

Materials needed:
Pottery with a diameter of 3⅛" (8cm) and a height of 2" (5cm)
* As the base has no drainage holes, add a medium to prevent root rot (➡p.80).

Plant 'Momobijin' toward the back and then *densirosulata* counterclockwise (1, 2). Next, plant *morganianum* and the smaller *densirosulata* in that order (3, 4). Using small plants builds density and results in a tighter composition.

Bottom

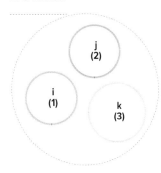

Succulents Used:
i: Graptopetalum mendozae (p.108)
j: Crassula 'Ivory Pagoda' (p.102)
k: Echeveria 'Iria' (p.86)

Materials needed:
Pottery with a diameter of 3½" (9cm) and a height of 2" (5cm)
* As the base has no drainage holes, add a medium to prevent root rot (➡p.80).

Plant *mendozae* on the left and 'Ivory Pagoda' toward the back (1, 2). Then, plant 'Iria' (3), leaving some gaps for a attractively natural finish.

TIP: Pinkish varieties were chosen for the pink containers, while pastel green varieties were used in the blue containers.

Combining Various Shades of Green

Pale green color may not be enough to express freshness. Mixing dark and light shades is key, as they'll set each other off and draw attention to each plant. Using plants with contrasting but complementary sizes, leaf shapes and other features keeps the arrangement interesting. The arrangement below also alternates tall plants with low-growing ones to create height differences.

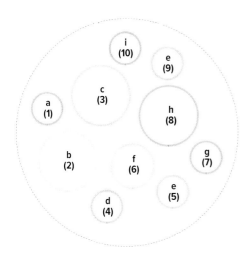

Succulents Used:
a: Kalanchoe scapigera (p.93)
b: Echeveria nicksana (p.89)
c: Sedeveria 'Harry Butterfield' (p.85)
d: Sedum makinoi (p.84)
e: Sedum selskianum (p.83)
f: Sedum 'Alice Evans' (p.84)
g: Echeveria spectabilis (p.86)
h: Echeveria 'Peach Pride' (p.88)
i: Sedum oryzifolium (p.83)
* Divide the Sedum selskianum.
* When planting in tight spaces, it's helpful to break apart the root ball and reduce the volume of the soil.

Materials needed:
Tin cake mold with a diameter of 6" (15cm) and a height of 3⅛" (8cm)
* Make drainage holes at the bottom (➜p.80).

Careful placement is key to arranging plants of different sizes. We started by making a rough plan for the larger plants, *nicksana*, 'Peach Pride', 'Alice Evans', and 'Harry Butterfield.'

From the left edge, plant *scapigera*, *nicksana*, and 'Harry Butterfield' at angles with the branch tips facing outward (1–3).

Plant *makinoi* and *selskianum* to spill over the edge (4, 5). Inside, plant 'Alice Evans' leaning forward (6).

Plant *spectabilis* and 'Peach Pride' (7, 8). Overall, planting smaller plants next to larger ones creates variation in height and color continuity.

Rotate the container and plant *selskianum* to overflow from the edge (9). Fill the remaining gaps with *oryzifolium* (10), and it's done.

TIP: The trailing makinoi in the foreground center becomes more dynamic when its branches intertwine with adjacent succulents, creating a natural appearance.

This pure white container sets off gray leaves that are charmingly tinged with color brought on by cool fall temperatures. Using plants that have been allowed to grow unrestrained adds a sense of movement to the arrangement's sense of serenity. Position the plants so that the colors are contrasting to add a sense of depth.

Combining Reddish Leaves

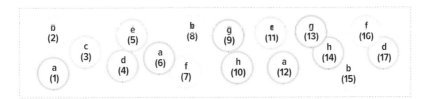

Succulents Used:

a: Sedum muscoideum (p.85)

b: Crassula 'Jade Necklace' (p.104)

c: Sedum prolifera (p.84)

d: Crassula volkensii (p.102)

e: Sedum reflexum 'Chameleon' (p.82)

f: Sedum burrito (p.83)

g: Crassula punctulata (p.103)

h: Crassula conjuncta (p.104)

Materials needed:

White iron container with dimensions of width 12" (30cm) x depth 2¾" (7cm) x height 3½" (9cm)

To achieve the natural beauty of different varieties blending together, divide all the plants except for 'Chameleon'. Be careful not to damage the roots; hold the base of the plant and divide slowly. The finer the roots, the more care is needed.

From left to right, plant muscoideum, 'Jade Necklace' and *prolifera*, ensuring that they are lying flat and leaning to the front left (1–3). Balance is important when it comes to the amount of foliage hanging from the edge of the container.

Tilt *volkensii*, 'Chameleon', and *muscoideum* to the left side and plant *burrito* diagonally to the front (4–7). Plant *muscoideum* to surround the *burrito*.

Plant 'Jade Necklace', *punctulata*, and *conjuncta* followed by *prolifera* (8–11). These plants form the center and highest section, so it's best to plant them completely upright

Plant *muscoideum*, *punctulata*, *conjuncta*, and 'Jade Necklace' leaning to the left side (12–15). Angle the seedlings more as you move toward the edge for a natural finish.

Plant *burrito* leaning to the left (16) and plant *volkensii* (17). As the arrangement gets nearer to completion, planting gets trickier, so dig deep into the soil so the roots will be firmly established.

TIP: Placing the center of the arrangement (the highest point) slightly to the right of the pot's center creates a relaxed, unconstrained expression.

Using a Pot Without Drainage Holes

While it's best to plant in pots with drainage holes, there are other ways to facilitate drainage. If your container has no holes, after watering generously, tilt the container to drain off excess water after a few minutes.

Making Holes

For materials like aluminum or tin, you can use nails to make holes. However, if you want to make holes in ceramics, you'll need a specialized drill, so it's best to have it done at a gardening store.

Materials needed:

Tin container, thick nails, hammer

Place a thick nail in the center of the bottom and hammer it to make a hole.

Repeat step 1 to make holes evenly over the bottom. Increase the number of holes depending on the size of the container.

Another convenient option

If you have a punch (middle),which can be found at home improvement stores, you can easily make larger holes.

Using Root Rot Preventative

If you want to use containers made of materials that can't be pierced, like glass or ceramics, use root rot preventatives. Mixing the right amount into the soil creates pathways for roots, water, and air while also suppressing bacteria. When using chemical preparations, always follow manufacturer directions and protect your eyes, skin and air passages.

Root rot preventatives can kill harmful bacteria (left). Another option is use additives to improve aeration, such as Perlite (right).

Regarding Surface Decoration for Pots

If the soil area appears too open, making your plants seem sparse, covering the surface with bright, natural materials can enhance the arrangement. Materials like akadama soil or potting stones of moderate size are recommended. Consider the plant's atmosphere and leaf color when choosing compatible materials.

You don't necessarily need special materials for surface decoration. The left arrangement (page 68) uses small akadama soil grains, while the right arrangement (page 72) uses lightweight stones (pumice) typically used for potting stones.

PART 3

A Catalog of the 250
Varieties Best
for Beginners

Sedum (Stonecrop)—Family Crassulaceae

Sedum palmeri

The lime-green leaves turn pinkish-red around the edges in winter, rather like a subtle touch of makeup. It's shrubby in nature and relatively tolerant of both heat and cold.

Sedum makinoi *'Ogon'*

This stonecrop's leaves are in various shades of golden green. These plants are resistant to cold and suitable for garden planting, such as between stepping stones. They spread horizontally as they grow, making them useful as ground cover.

Sedum adolphi *'Golden Glow'*

The leaf tips flush red in the cold, becoming a beautiful orange color. Shrubby in nature, when it grows upward and becomes heavy, it looks as if it's tilting its head.

Sedum pachyphyllum

As fall deepens, the light green leaf tips turn a charming pink. Placing it in direct sunlight and watering and fertilizing it moderately will enhance its vivid colors. It grows upward while branching out.

Sedum rubrotinctum *'Aurora'*

The glossy green leaves turn pink in the cold, creating a beautiful contrast. It's a variegated species of "Rainbow Sedum." When it grows, the lower leaves fall off, so it's advisable to prune it. It propagates through cuttings.

Sedum reflexum *'Chameleon'*

This plant's blue-gray slender leaves branch out as it grows upward, and the entire plant turns pink in the cold. There's also a white variegation of this plant.

Sedum multiceps

Shrubby in nature, as it grows, the lower leaves on the stems fall off and the stems become woody, with only fine leaves growing at the tips, resembling a small bonsai pine. The leaf tips turn red in the cold.

Sedum album *'Coral Carpet'*

It has oval-shaped, chubby small leaves that spread out like creeping vines. It goes from deep green to a chic reddish-brown during the fall. Highly resistant to drought. It can be propagated through division and cuttings.

Sedum makinoi *'Aurea'*

The vivid yellow-green small leaves overlapping each other create a carpet effect. This variety spreads out like a creeping vine and is suitable for ground cover. It's susceptible to moisture, so once it becomes dense, it's best to trim it for better air circulation.

Sedum mexicanum

The lime-green leaves become a vivid yellow-green as it gets cold. It's resistant to cold and can handle a bit more water and shade than most Sedum. This, combined with its creeper-like tendencies, makes it a great choice for ground cover.

Sedum spathulifolium ssp. pruinosum
'Cape Blanco'

The bluish-silver small leaves overlap like a single flower. It's cold-resistant but dislikes heat, so it should be kept in a well-ventilated place with moderate dryness in summer. Also known simply as "Cape Blanco Sedum."

Sedum oryzifolium f. albiflora

Called "Shirobana Taitogome" in its native Japan, it grows upward in a fluffy manner, but when the top becomes heavy, it droops and spreads like a creeper. It can also be grown in hanging baskets.

Sedum burrito

A very popular trailing succulent. The clustered small leaves stand up and droop due to their weight, and fall off easily. Pruning to increase the number of branches encourages clumping. An easy one to propagate through leaves and stem sections.

Sedum spurium *'Stephanie Gold'*

Its green leaves with serrated edges are characteristic, and the stems spread horizontally along the ground. As the temperature drops, they gradually turn reddish-brown. It's cold-resistant and suitable for garden planting.

Sedum versadense

The thick, hairy leaves grow densely and form clusters. Since the stems grow upward during the growing season, pruning should be done before or early in the season. In winter, they turn red on the underside of the leaves, and can be stunningly vibrant.

Sedum morganianum

The refreshing green leaves hanging down are especially beautiful when planted in a tall pot, where their charm shines. If the branches grow too long, trim them back. Be careful as the leaves come of easily when touched.

Sedum treleasei

The chubby, fleshy leaves have a white powdery surface. Since it grows upward in a shrubby manner, occasional pruning is needed to maintain its shape. In cold weather, the tips of the leaves turn pink.

Sedum spurium *'Dragon's Blood'*

Bright green in summer and flowering in summer, its leaves work their way into a vibrant reddish-purple as the weather turns cold. They are resistant to both heat and cold, making them excellent garden accents.

Sedum rubrotinctum

This is the much-loved "Jellybean Plant." The green leaves turn red as the temperature drops, and their fall to winter foliage features even brighter and deeper hues. They propagate easily through stem or leaf cuttings.

Sedum dasyphyllum var. alternum

The bluish-gray mall leaves turn a beautiful purple in winter. As they grow, they fluff up and spread upward and sideways, creating volume. In spring, flower stems extend, producing white flowers.

Sedum *'Alice Evans'*

Among sedums, this is a relatively large variety. Its lime green leaves take on a yellowish-green hue when it gets cold, and the leaf tips turn red. Offshoots form around the rosette base. It grows quickly and is cold-resistant.

Sedum makinoi f. variegata

A variegated species of Japanese stonecrop. Its bright green leaves are edged in cream. The spreading new shoots are especially lovely. It is low-growing, and prefers somewhat milder weather than most stonecrops, though it is resistant to heat and cold.

Sedum lineare f. variegata

A standing type of stonecrop with green, slender, elongated small leaves edged in white. The white spots turn pink as the cold intensifies. When it grows larger and the plant becomes messy, pruning is recommended.

Sedum brevifolium

It has countless tiny blue-gray round leaves that grow upward. It is low-growing and compact, resistant to cold but susceptible to summer humidity. It should be grown in well-ventilated conditions.

Sedum prolifera

Forming rosettes with thick, bluish-white small leaves, they turn a gentle pink in winter. They produce many runners from the sides, adding a pleasing touch. They are relatively resistant to heat and cold.

Sedum lucidum

The glossy, chubby, round green leaves turn red at the tips as the weather gets colder. It grows upright, with slow growth. It's resistant to cold and drought but dislikes hot and humid summers.

Sedum makinoi

The refreshing sight of overlapping yellowish-green round leaves characterizes this stonecrop. As a creeper, it can be grown in hanging baskets. Care should be taken not to overwater.

Sedum adolphi

One of the representative species of golden Sedum, with its characteristic coppery yellow leaf color. It grows upright, branching out as it matures. As fall deepens, it subtly turns from yellow to orange in color.

Sedum muscoideum

This variety's grainy green leaves take on a subdued purple hue in fall. Rather than creeping along the ground, it grows diagonally upward, giving it a dynamic appearance. It's relatively resistant to both heat and cold.

Sedum rubens

It exudes a charming resemblance to a smaller version of *adolphi*. Its yellow-green leaves turn orange during the fall season. The red stems are also striking. Rather than growing in clumps, it cascades downward. It works well in hanging baskets.

CLOSE RELATIVE OF SEDUM Sedum reflexum belongs to the Crassulaceae family, Sedum genus

Sedum rubrotinctum *'Red Berry'*

A viviparous species of "Rainbow Stonecrop." It gets its name from the berry-like clusters that form on the leaf tips late in the fall, as well as for the berry red color of its leaves in winter. It's resistant to both cold and drought.

Hylotelephium sieboldii

A variety of Japanese stonecrop, it can grow outdoors throughout the year. Its bluish-green leaves are rounded, edged with pink that deepens in summer, with the color spreading throughout the leaves as the weather turns colder. The stems grow diagonally and eventually form clumps.

HYBRID OF SEDUM AND ECHEVERIA Sedeveria belongs to the Crassulaceae family, Sedeveria genus

Sedeveria *'Yellow Humbert'*

This variety has chubby, slender leaves that turn orange to pink at the tips during fall. As it's a shrubby variety, it's a good choice for rock gardens.

Sedeveria *'Harry Butterfield'*

Nicknamed "Super Donkey Tail," this variety cascades downward after standing upright. It has beautiful powder green leaves. Be sure to shield it against summer humidity

Echeveria, of the Crassulaceae Family and Echeveria Genus

Echeveria *'Arctic Ice'*

Its bluish-green leaves are adorned with a white powder. In summer, beware of leaf scorch and manage with partial shade and slightly dry conditions. In winter, the leaf tips take on a faint pink hue.

Echeveria elegans *'Alba'*

This variety has a relatively tight rosette shape, with translucent milky pale green leaves whose tips turn pink when exposed to cold. It's a slow grower. Move it indoors before frost.

Echeveria *'Ilia'*

The pale green leaves turn a translucent milky white in winter. It produces numerous offsets and grows densely layered. During summer, it should be managed in partial shade with slightly dry conditions.

Echeveria *'Emerald Ripple'*

Its beautiful emerald green leaves, from which its name originates, have a pink hue at the tips. It's relatively resistant to both cold and heat. As the cold intensifies, it turns red, and the fall foliage is beautiful.

Echeveria *'Autumn Flame'*

Its impressively glossy, deep wine-red large leaves with undulating edges are striking. The flowers are red and bloom from spring to summer. In winter, it should be managed in a location with temperatures above 41°F (5°C). Its impressively glossy, deep wine-red large leaves with undulating edges are striking. The flowers are red and bloom from spring to summer. In winter, it should be managed in a location with temperatures above 41°F (5°C).

Echeveria *'Hanaikada'*

Its vibrant reddish-purple leaves are eye-catching. It grows shrubby. As it gets colder, the leaves intensify in color and become glossy. Exposing it to sunlight enhances the beauty of its fall foliage. In summer, it should be managed in partial shade with slightly dry conditions.

Echeveria *'Orion'*

Its purple-gray leaves, adorned with white powder, have slightly pink edges. A variety born in the Netherlands, it turns red in deep fall, ultimately taking on a translucent purple color.

Echeveria *'Ginbugen'*

A beautiful variety of bluish milky-white color with white powder all over. As a rosette type, it produces offsets from the base as it grows larger. It flowers in orange blossoms from spring to summer.

Echeveria spectabilis

Its dark green leaves turn red at the tips in cold weather, creating a dramatic effect. As it has a tendency to extend its stem upward, it's advisable to trim it back once the lower leaves have fallen and become woody. It can be propagated by stem cuttings.

Echeveria peacockii subsessilis

Variant of the large-leaved *peacockii*. The blue-gray leaves with pink edges are graceful. As it gets colder, the pink edges become more pronounced. It grows to a considerable size and forms clusters.

Echeveria agavoides

Also called Echeveria 'Jade Point'. This variety forms a tight, dense rosette. When exposed to cold, the red of its leaf tips extends to the entire plant. It's relatively resilient to both heat and cold. It grows vigorously and large.

Echeveria shaviana

The rosette-shaped leaves have finely undulating edges. With a white powder on the leaf surface, the pink to purple gradient is glamorous. It dislikes summer heat, so provide shade. It can be propagated by stem cuttings.

Echeveria *'Joan Daniel'*

Highlighted by red edges and a central red stripe on the underside of the leaf, complementing the green leaf color. As fall deepens, the leaves gradually turn red. Since the leaves are prone to moisture, water should be applied onto the soil only.

Echeveria *'Serrana'*

The chic reddish-brown leaves are slender and pointed. It blooms orange flowers from spring to summer, and in winter, it turns a deep chocolate color. It's relatively resilient to both heat and cold.

Echeveria *'Takasago no Okina'*

A large species with gently undulating leaves overlapping like cabbage. In fall, as the temperature drops, it turns vivid red. It's susceptible to waterlogging during prolonged rain. It grows vigorously and quickly forms stems.

Echeveria chihuahuaensis

With thick, powdery white leaves, it forms beautiful rosettes. The pink-tipped leaves are cute. During the fall foliage, the pink becomes more pronounced. It grows slowly and can be propagated by leaf cuttings.

Echeveria elegans

Characterized by the translucent edges and white powder of its pale green leaves. In winter, it turns slightly pink. Propagate by increasing offsets to form clusters and grow slowly.

Echeveria *'Deresina'*

The rosette-shaped leaves, stacked with thick silver-blue foliage, are very beautiful, turning pink overall as it gets colder. It can withstand temperatures down to about 41°F (5°C) in winter. Protect from frost and cold winds.

Echeveria *'Domingo'*

The leaves are thin, with a beautiful light blue hue covered in white powder. As it gets colder, the edges of the leaves turn pink, adding elegance. The stems grow upward, and offsets cluster, so repotting and pruning are beneficial.

Echeveria *'Neon Breakers'*

Large frilly leaves with "fluorescent" pink edges, making them stand out. In winter, the entire plant turns reddish-purple, adding vibrancy. It can grow up to about 8" (20cm) in diameter. Sun exposure enhances its coloration.

Echeveria *'Nobaranosei'*

The rosette of densely layered powder-blue leaves is reminiscent of wild roses. In winter, it takes on a faint pink hue, and the leaf tips turn a bright red during peak foliage. It blooms orange flowers that contrast beautifully with the leaves.

Echeveria *'Powder Blue'*

The pink edges embellish the leaf color vividly. The foliage turns red during fall, with the leaf tips taking on a deeper shade. The leaves are thin and greatly enlarge during the growing season. It readily produces offsets.

Echeveria *'Hakuhou'*

A hybrid originating from Japan. It boasts thick, large blue-green leaves with hints of pink, adding elegance. The fall foliage, turning pink or orange, is also stunning.

Echeveria *'Pink Crystal'*

The light green leaves are edged with pink, a subtle and charming bit of color. The winter foliage turns a gentle pink. It dislikes the humid summer heat.

Echeveria *'Perle Von Nurnberg'*

The beautiful purple leaves deepen in redness and color intensity as it gets colder, becoming even more elegant. The rounded leaves have a gentle inward curl, adding softness. Pruning when it grows tall is advisable.

Echeveria *'Peach Pride'*

Its prominent feature is the large, round and compact rosette with pink-tipped, pointed leaves. During fall, the upper parts of the leaves turn a peachy blush color. Creates offsets as it grows.

Echeveria *'Black Knight'*

One of the *Echeveria affinis* (Black Echeveria) whose glossy dark leaves can appear anywhere from deep purple to deep brown. The leaves are fleshy and the white translucent leaf tips add a sense of emphasis. While there's little change in leaf color throughout the seasons, good sunlight enhances its hues.

Echeveria *'Black Rose'*

The radiating arrangement of leaves that can appear in a variety of shades from chocolate to burgundy. The leaves are thick and somewhat matte.. Exposure to cold intensifies their red hue. As it grows, offsets develop at the base.

Echeveria *'Princess Pearl'*

The thin green leaves, outlined in pink with frills, give an elegant impression. The fall foliage is also beautiful, turning entirely red. As it grows, the stem becomes erect, and offsets emerge at the base.

Echeveria *'Blue Prince'*

The slender bluish-purple leaves form a graceful rosette, giving off an expansive impression and a unique personality. It blooms reddish-orange flowers from spring to summer. Be cautious as water tends to accumulate in the center of the leaves.

Echeveria *'Prism'*

The mint-green leaves with pink tips create an impressive and beautiful rosette, resembling a large rose. In winter, the pink color at the leaf tips intensifies. Shade it from intense summer sun, and be sure to protect it from frost in winter.

Echeveria *'Mallow'*

This variety has chic olive-hued leaves that are somewhat pointed. Their color leans toward crimson as temperatures change. Insufficient sunlight can cause color fading, so ensure it receives an adequate amount of sunlight. Prune when it grows too tall.

Echeveria nicksana

The rosettes formed by bluish-green leaves have a well-defined shape and a gentle presence. In winter, the leaf tips take on a reddish hue. Pruning when it grows upward and propagating through stem cuttings are options.

Echeveria *'Laurinze'*

The pale blue leaves with white powder and pink edges exude elegance. The rosette shape is beautiful and delicate, yet resilient. Be cautious of excessive moisture in summer, and avoid water accumulation on the leaves. The fall foliage is also stunning.

Echeveria lilacina

"Lilacina" means "lilac-colored," and its leaves indeed sport a pale purple hue with a powdery texture. While the leaf shape is unique, the rosette form is exquisite. If temperatures drop below 41°F (5°C), move it indoors.

Echeveria *'Lola'*

A crossbreed between *lilacina* and 'Deresina'. It forms a beautiful rosette with a light, translucent leaf coloration. It grows large overall and produces offsets that cluster around it. In summer, provide partial shade and good ventilation.

Haworthia, a Genus in the Family Asphodelaceae

SOFT-LEAVED VARIETIES

Haworthia cooperi var. pilifera

Cooperi variety with elongated leaves. They have relatively large windows at their tips, which become transparent. If exposed to too much sunlight, they turn purple and lose color. Shade is necessary in summer. They produce offsets at the base and clump together.

Haworthia umbraticola

Compact grassy appearance with thick, short leaves. The leaves are dark green, becoming transparent toward the tips. They grow vigorously and clump densely at the base. They can be propagated by division.

Haworthia cooperi var. truncata

The short, round leaves give the appearance of sparkling windows spreading at the tips. A popular miniature variety with densely packed leaves. Depending on sunlight exposure, the deep green leaves can turn red to purple.

Haworthia truncate

When the leaves are symmetrically extended, they resemble fans when viewed from the side. Their windowed tips give the impression of having been abruptly cut. They grow slowly and require more light compared to other varieties.

Haworthia cooperi

Its leaves unfold into an orderly rosette shape, and their surfaces feature the large jelly-like windows characteristic of so many *Haworthia*. They produce many offsets at the base to form clumps.

Haworthia 'Black Splendens'

Small to medium-sized species. Its thick, pointed leaves form a dome shape, and the striped patterns within the window area have a glossy, juicy appearance. Depending on the season and light intensity, the leaves can range from purple to blackish in color.

Haworthia turgida

Due to their wide leaves, the window area is also broad, creating a crisp and refreshing overall appearance. The curve of the leave tip lends the overall plant a lively shape. They produce offsets and form clumps.

Haworthia cuspidata

This variety features chubby triangular leaves with small windows at the tips. The leaves form a tight, neatly arranged rosette. The refreshing light green color lasts throughout the year. This variety produces many offsets.

Haworthia picta

The *picta* has triangular windows at the top of its radiating leaves. The name comes from the white speckled patterns that float on the blue-green windows. If light is insufficient, the white color fades, and the leaves elongate.

Haworthia bolusii × Haworthia bolusii var. aranea

A hybrid of *bolusii*, with fine white hairs extending from the tips and edges of the leaves, and *aranea*, with white hairs covering the plant. Be cautious of excessive humidity in summer. It's advisable to provide shade and reduce watering until fall.

Haworthia *'Mirrorball'*

The pointed leaves are short, with short white hairs growing along the edges. The clear veins on both sides of the leaves are distinctly visible. Under good sunlight conditions, they take on a purple hue. They produce offsets prolifically.

Haworthia *'Mirrorball'* × **Haworthia bolusii**

A hybrid of 'Mirrorball' with beautiful translucent windows and *bolusii* with white hairs at the leaf tips and edges. The short, pointed leaves are densely packed. Keep them slightly dry in summer.

Haworthia *'Murasaki Obtusa'* × **Haworthia cooperi var. venusta**

This hybrid gets its purple tinge from the 'Murasaki Obtusa' and its shape and fluffy white leaf hairs from the *venusta*. A slow grower.

Haworthia ramose

The overlapping and coiling leaves resemble blooming roses. The leaves grow slowly and do not open further than you see here. Accumulated water between the leaves can cause damage from excessive moisture, so be sure to confine watering to the soil only.

Haworthia rosea

This variety features an elegant arrangement of leaves with semi-transparent windows tinged with yellow-green. They turn pink and become vibrant when light and moisture are lacking. They tend to produce offsets easily. They prefer slightly strong light.

HARD-LEAVED VARIETIES

Haworthia attenuate

Known "Zebra Cactus" for the white mottled patterns on the back of its sharp, hard green leaves. The leaf color turns red when the weather gets colder. They should be grown in slightly bright, partial shade.

Haworthia *'Super Big Band'*

Relatively hardy and easy to grow. They prefer well-ventilated partial shade in summer, as excessive sunlight can turn them reddish-brown.

Haworthia reinwardtii var. archibaldiae

The backs of the pointed, dark green leaves are rounded and adorned with white spots, resembling stars. They grow upward and produce offsets from the base, forming clumps. They are easy to cultivate.

Kalanchoe, Genus of Crassulaceae Family

RABBIT SERIES

Kalanchoe tomentosa f. nigromarginatas
The fluffy leaves growing in pairs on the stem resemble rabbit ears, making it a popular series. The edges of the small leaves are brown, giving an overall dark impression. It grows upward while branching out.

Kalanchoe tomentosa f. nigromarginatas *'Kurotoji'*
The thick leaves, covered with fine hairs, feel like felt. Brown spots border the edges of the leaves. When it gets cold, the leaf color changes to a yellowish hue. Accumulated water on the leaves can cause leaf scorch.

Kalanchoe tomentosa *'Golden Girl'*
The leaves covered with white hairs appear golden. Spots along the edges serve as accents. Growth is slow and compact. Keep it in temperatures above 41°F (5°C). Also known as 'Golden Rabbit'.

Kalanchoe tomentosa *Shirousagi'*
Leaves adorned with short white hairs have a pure, snow-like charm. The patterns along the edges are understated. They may take on a slightly yellowish-white color in summer. Avoid strong sunlight and high temperatures in midsummer. Cut back on watering in winter.

Kalanchoe tomentosa
The bluish-green leaves are covered with fine hairs, and chestnut spots border them. They are sensitive to high humidity and cold, requiring temperatures above 41°F (5°C) in winter.

Kalanchoe eriophylla
The whiteness of the leaves is its characteristic feature. The fine hairs are long and dense. The leaves are small and grow in branching patterns. They tend to elongate in poor sunlight conditions.

Kalanchoe tomentosa *'Teddy Bear'*
The brown-edged leaves are elongated, with the color becoming darker toward the tips, creating a beautiful gradient. Be cautious of direct sunlight and excessive moisture in summer.

Kalanchoe tomentosa *'Star'*
Named for the dot-like patterns along the edges of the leaves, resembling stars that form a beautiful contrast with the bluish-green backdrop. In summer, they may turn slightly cream-colored. Avoid exposing them to prolonged rain.

Kalanchoe marmorata

The striking red-purple mottled pattern catches the eye. There are gentle incisions along the edges. During the fall foliage season, the leaves change color and the patterns become even more vivid. It is sensitive to cold, so it should be moved indoors where sunlight enters during winter.

Kalanchoe bracteata

The spoon-shaped leaves covered in white powder grow upward while branching out. Its natural tree-like form is beautiful. The leaves are easily detached when touched. It is sensitive to cold.

Kalanchoe tubiflora

With its unique form of elongated leaves extending in all directions and producing offsets at the tips, this plant features a pink base with black patterns, which is quite innovative. It prefers sunlight but should be placed in partial shade during summer. It dislikes cold and humidity.

Kalanchoe daigremontiana

Numerous offsets emerge along the serrated edges of the leaves, taking root when they fall onto the soil and growing. It is resilient to heat but dislikes excessive moisture. Ensure good airflow during summer.

Kalanchoe fedtschenkoi

The flat leaves adorned with jagged edges colored in pink grow upward in a layered fashion. They turn reddish-purple during the fall. Exposing them to sunlight maintains their color without elongation. It is sensitive to cold.

Kalanchoe scapigera

The fan-shaped leaves stand upright, growing upward. They turn from deep green to yellowish-green during the fall, with the tips reddening. During winter, they should be placed in sunny indoor locations.

Kalanchoe beharensis

A large and resilient variety. The velvet-like leaves covered in fine hairs have a distinctive and dynamic shape. The light brownish new leaves turn grayish-green as they mature.

Kalanchoe orgyalis

The leaves, velvety with brown tops and silver undersides, have a fashionable and unique appearance. Although slow-growing, they become woody and shrub-like when mature. They are sensitive to cold and require good airflow.

Kalanchoe pumila

The silver leaves covered with white powder have incisions along the edges. They extend upward while branching out, giving a dynamic sensation as if dancing. If the plant becomes disorderly, it should be pruned.

Kalanchoe *'Phoenix'*

Long, narrow leaves with distinctive black-purple patterns. Numerous offsets appear along the leaf edges, and they multiply rapidly when they naturally fall off. Insufficient sunlight dulls the leaf color. Keep it relatively dry in summer and winter.

Kalanchoe humilis

The round, bluish-green leaves with reddish-purple stripes give a wild impression. Offsets emerge and form clusters. Excessive moisture can obscure the patterns. It dislikes both summer humidity and cold.

Kalanchoe grandiflora *'Fuyumomiji'*

The deeply incised leaves resemble maple leaves. Green leaves turn orange and become vibrant as temperatures drop. Prune and tidy up if they grow too long. It's sensitive to cold, so manage it indoors during winter.

Kalanchoe behalensis *'Fang'*

Large leaves covered with short hairs have a velvety texture. The fang-like protrusions on the underside of the leaves give this variety its name. Growth is slow, and as it grows larger, lower leaves fall off and become woody. It's sensitive to excessive moisture, so ensure good ventilation.

Kalanchoe beharensis *'Whiteleaf'*

Both leaves and stems are covered with fine white hairs, giving a velvety texture. The leaf edges are serrated and gently undulate. It grows upward and enlarges. Sunlight is necessary, but be cautious of leaf scorch.

Kalanchoe millotii

Covered with white short hairs and serrated edges, the light green leaves have a felt-like texture. It dislikes cold but turns brownish in fall as temperatures drop. It gradually grows taller.

Kalanchoe gastonis-bonnieri

Named for its resemblance to the summer plumage of the capercaillie bird. Leaves can grow up to about 20" (50cm) in size. Offsets form at the tips of leaves and multiply. During winter, it should be kept indoors in a sunny location.

Euphorbia, Spurge Family

Euphorbia anoplia

With a cactus-like appearance, it has intricate striped patterns on its body, giving it a rich texture. Growth is slow but extends upward, with ridges (where the thorns are) increasing and changing shape. It propagates via underground stems, producing offsets.

Euphorbia *'Obesablow'*

A Japanese hybrid, this variety's spherical succulent form produces numerous offsets and grows upward, with the base becoming woody. Offsets can be separated from the parent plant and propagated through stem cuttings. Caution should be exercised due to the toxic white sap.

Euphorbia oncoclada f. cristata

A cristata variety of Euphorbia with slender cylindrical stems. Growth points on each stem are connected in bands, growing in a fan-like shape. Adorable offsets emerge at the tip. Requires bright shade during summer.

Euphorbia *'Kaimagyoku'*

It sports elongated leaves densely clustered at the apex, giving it a humorous appearance. The bumpy texture on the trunk is due to fallen leaves. During prolonged rainy periods, ensure good ventilation. Winter care involves keeping it in a bright indoor location.

Euphorbia enopla

Covered in long red thorns that adorn its entire surface. Exposing it to ample sunlight enhances the color of the thorns. While robust, excessive moisture can lead to root rot. Reduce watering in winter and manage it indoors.

Euphorbia pulvinata

Gradually erecting its stem and easily forming offsets, creating clusters. During spring growth, it produces elongated leaves from the apex, accompanied by red thorns. Extremely hardy and easy to care for.

Euphorbia mammillaris *'Variegata'*

Adorable pink thorns adorn its white body. It produces offsets prolifically. With suitable conditions such as sunlight, moisture, and temperature fluctuations, it turns pink in winter.

Euphorbia *'Biseigyoku'*

Resembling a spherical cactus. As it grows, the ridges increase, extending upward. As it matures, offsets continually emerge from the base. It thrives in well-lit areas.

Euphorbia razafindratsirae

A tuberous species native to Madagascar, spreading branches in all directions. Its green leaves with undulating edges are not succulent. Its pale yellow bracts are also beautiful. It can grow to a size of about 10–12″ (25–30cm) in diameter.

Cactus, Cactaceae Family

Pilosocereus azureus

A columnar cactus with a bluish-green skin adorned with yellow spines. As it grows, the woolly areoles become prominent. During winter, it should be kept somewhat dry.

Parodia magnifica

With a crown-like form, its slender gold-colored spines are striking. In summer, it blooms yellow flowers at the apex. As it matures, it becomes cylindrical, producing offsets from the base and forming clusters.

Espostoa lanata

Impressive with its white fluffy hairs, this columnar cactus grows slowly upward. During summer, it should be kept somewhat dry in a well-ventilated semi-shaded area. Exposed to rain, its hairs get dirty, so it should be moved under eaves.

Mammillaria canelensis

Globuar and densely-spined, this cactus produces pink flowers from spring to summer. Requires ample sunlight and good ventilation. Insufficient sunlight can lead to poor shape.

Cereus variabilis f. monstrosus

Its brown spines are soft. Though belonging to the *Cereus* genus, a group of columnar cacti, it repeatedly branches and forms a unique tree-like structure with multiple petrified growth points.

Echinocactus grusonii

Featuring large and sharp yellow spines, it maintains a spherical shape as it grows. It prefers sunlight, with insufficient light leading to weak spines. Requires temperatures above 41°F (5°C) even in winter. Below this, red spots appear on the skin.

Echinopsis calochlora

Maintaining a round shape while growing, it produces offsets at the base, forming clusters. Prolonged dampness, such as during heavy rain, can cause root rot. In summer, it blooms large white flowers. Avoid direct sunlight in midsummer.

Espostoa guentheri

A columnar cactus with short, beautiful yellow spines. Relatively hardy but slow-growing. Dislikes humid summer conditions. During summer, keep it in a well-ventilated place, avoiding strong light and excessive moisture.

Espostoa melanostele

Covered in long white hairs with protruding sharp spines, this columnar cactus should be watered at the base to prevent the hairs from getting dirty. Requires ample sunlight and good ventilation. Dislikes cold temperatures.

Mammillaria elongate

Small in size, its radiating yellow spines give it the nickname the "Gold Lace" cactus. It grows quickly, producing offsets at the base and forming clusters. Be cautious of high humidity and ensure good airflow for cultivation.

Gymnocalycium saglionis

Characterized by its bumpy spherical shape and long, thick spines. It stores water in its thick roots. Dislikes strong sunlight and prefers partial shading. During winter, manage it near a sunny window with almost no watering.

Echinopsis eyriesii

Short spines are its distinctive feature. As the spherical shape matures, it becomes cylindrical. It grows quickly and produces many offsets. As the plant matures, it blooms white to pale yellow flowers. It can survive outdoors in winter if frost is avoided.

Opuntia debreczyi

Grows in a fan-like shape, with overlapping stems resembling stacked fans. Its deep green color is striking. Insufficient sunlight leads to elongation and deformity. It is resilient and easy to cultivate, tolerating cold temperatures well.

Astrophytum ornatum

Adorned with white specks resembling stars on a spherical body. Its long, sharp spines and impressive spiral-like appearance are attractive. Prefers sunlight. Avoid complete withholding of water even in winter.

Pachycereus pringlei

A columnar cactus covered in spines, with multiple ribs bearing white woolly areoles. New spines change from orange to brown. Dislikes cold temperatures.

Echinocereus rigidissimus var. rubrispinus

Vibrant purple spines add a touch of glamour. Covered with fine spines overall, they are not painful to touch. A small-sized columnar cactus that produces offsets from the base. Sun exposure enhances the coloration of the spines.

Oreocereus neocelsianus

Adorned with abundant long white hairs and sharp yellow spines. A petite columnar cactus with a decorative appeal. It blooms pink flowers in summer. Provide partial shade with good airflow during midsummer.

Rebutia deminuta

Produces offsets abundantly, forming clusters. Flower buds emerge from the base and areola crests, blooming orange-tinted flowers in spring. It is sensitive to strong direct sunlight. During summer, place it in a bright, well-ventilated partial shade.

Agave, Agave Family

Agave isthmensis

The serrated silver-green leaves are stunning. Tipped with thick spines, they exude a powerful presence. The symmetrical rosette shape is also beautiful. It's highly drought-tolerant.

Agave victoriae-reginae

Radiating slender green leaves with elegant white markings. It produces offsets, forming clusters. Resilient to heat and cold but sensitive to overwatering. Avoid direct sunlight in summer and frost in winter.

Agave leopoldii

The sharp leaves spread out radially from the center, adorned with curling white threads along their edges, creating a dynamic and beautiful appearance. Highly drought-tolerant but prone to elongation in low light conditions.

Agave pygmaea *'Dragon Toes'*

Named for the fine thorns along the leaf edges, resembling "dinosaur toes." The silver-gray leaves of this large species are also beautiful. When the parent plant matures, it produces offsets around it. Avoid frost in winter.

Agave stricta

The long, graceful green leaves spread out vigorously like a fountain. Relatively tolerant to cold, it can be grown outdoors year-round west of the Kanto region. Pay attention to avoiding excess moisture. Good airflow and sunlight are important.

Agave bracteosa *'Monterrey Frost'*

Long, flexible slender leaves with no thorns, adorned with white markings along the edges, giving a refreshing feel. A small-sized species. As it grows, the number of leaves increases, forming a rounded shape. The leaves are fragile but resilient to cold and drought.

Agave *'Blue Ember'*

The contrast between the blue-green leaves and the magenta serrations along the edges is stunning. Highly drought-tolerant but susceptible to excess moisture. Standing water in the pot saucer can damage the roots.

Agave *'Blue Glow'*

Beautiful brown-edged blue-green leaves with fine thorns along the edges. Exposure to sunlight enhances the leaf color. Be cautious as water droplets on the leaves can leave white marks upon evaporation.

Agave horrida

Along the glossy dark green edges, white and brown thorns dance, creating a unique appearance. Resilient to heat and cold, suitable for ground planting as well. Avoid overwatering and ensure good airflow.

Aloe, Asphodelaceae

Aloe eximia

A species recently discovered in the high mountains of Madagascar. Its blue-green leaves with a white powdery coating are beautiful. It grows with sharp, twisting leaves and is relatively cold-hardy.

Aloe capitata

The striking red-edged serrated thorns bordering the leaves are impressive. The vibrant green leaves take on a purple hue when temperatures drop, making them beautiful. With a cold tolerance of 32°F (0°C), it should be kept in a bright indoor space with minimal watering during winter.

Aloe suprafoliata

Its symmetrical, slender leaves spreading out stylishly are charming. As the leaves grow, they curve downward due to their weight. During winter, it should be kept near a sunny window with minimal watering.

Aloe 'Firebird'

The delicate, beautiful slender leaves with white spots as accents often branch out and cluster. In fall, it extends long flower stalks, producing orange flowers. During winter, when temperatures drop below 41°F (5°C), it should be kept indoors in a sunny spot.

Aloe ferox

With large, sharp thorns on thick leaves, it grows into a bushy plant. As it grows upward, the lower leaves dry out and become woody. It should be kept in a sunny and well-ventilated area, preferably where temperatures don't drop below 41°F (5°C).

Aloe peglerae

Its thick, succulent blue-green leaves with sharp edges curl inward, forming beautiful rosettes as they grow. The small red thorns add to its beauty. During winter, it should be kept indoors to prevent freezing.

RELATED TO ALOE

Aloidendron, Asphodelaceae

Aloe hereroensis

This aloe features thick leaves with spots. Young plants spread their leaves horizontally, but as they grow, they form rosettes. It grows slowly and prefers plenty of sunlight.

Aloe ramosissima

Its leaves grow upward, extending as it grows taller, often branching out and becoming bushy. The lower leaves dry out and become woody, resulting in a compact plant. Strong sunlight in midsummer can cause leaf scorch.

Aloidendron dichotomum

Formerly classified under Aloe genus, it can grow up to 11 yd (10 meters) tall in its native Africa. Even young plants can become tree-like with age. It thrives in strong sunlight and tolerates cold relatively well.

Lithops, Aizoaceae

Lithops lesliei *'Albinica'*

The vibrant yellow hues across the entire "window" contrast beautifully with the bluish-green of the plant. It tends to cluster and produces white flowers in fall.

Lithops bella

With a rounded, heart-like appearance on the top, its brown branch-like patterns on the "window" are vivid. It readily offsets and clusters. White flowers bloom in fall.

Lithops karasmontana *'Top Red'*

Characterized by a flat top with vivid red intricate patterns, it often offsets with repeated shedding. It requires some shade in summer and minimal watering during the rainy season to summer.

Lithops aucampiae

Its reddish-brown skin's top surface features dark brown intricate patterns. It sheds well, making it easy to propagate. Yellow flowers bloom in fall. It dislikes high humidity and prefers minimal watering in summer. It's cold-tolerant.

Lithops julii ssp. fulleri

Smooth pink-beige skin with red-brown windows adorned with prominent crack patterns that catch the eye. White flowers bloom in fall.

Lithops lesliei var. hornii

The flat top is covered with fine brown patterns, and it has shallow cracks. Yellow flowers bloom in fall. It dislikes high temperatures and humidity. Minimal watering is advised from the rainy season to summer.

RELATED TO LITHOPS

Rapidaria, Aizoaceae

Lithops julii ssp. fulleri *'Fullergreen'*

A *fulleri* that has turned green due to pigment loss. Its refreshing emerald green appearance is striking. It blooms white flowers in fall, but insufficient moisture during flowering may affect blooming.

Lithops julii ssp. fulleri

A purple variant with deep red-purple crack patterns on its purple skin. It's a popular variety. It requires almost no watering in summer and should be watered sparingly as fall approaches. It blooms white flowers in fall.

Lapidaria margaretae

Also known as the "Karoo Rose." Lapidaria is a monotypic genus. It requires shade and minimal watering during summer, blooming a yellow flower in fall.

Rhipsalis, Cactus Family

Rhipsalis elliptica

Its broad leaf-like stems branch out and sprawl freely. Intense sunlight turns the green leaves into a chic reddish-brown. In spring, clusters of white tiny flowers bloom along the edges of the stems.

Rhipsalis caciero

Its thread-like stems branch out, gracefully extending and spreading like a green shower, becoming voluminous. Pruning in spring for better airflow helps prevent excessive moisture.

Rhipsalis capilliformis

With cylindrical delicate stems branching out while hanging down, it exudes a soft charm. New shoots are light green, gradually darkening over time. Avoid direct sunlight and provide shelter during prolonged rain.

Rhipsalis kirbergii

Its slender and angular stems repeatedly branch out, creating a cascading, impactful presence. It prefers bright shade. Even when wilted due to drought, it quickly revives with watering. Keep indoors above 41°F (5°C) in winter.

Rhipsalis cereuscula

Its bright green stems, resembling grains of rice, freely extend in a delicate manner. Occasionally, they extend long stems, which then undergo repeated branching. Be cautious of excessive moisture.

Rhipsalis neves-armondii

Its translucent cylindrical stems branch out well, spreading out like sparklers. As they elongate, they start to droop. With growth, pale yellow tiny flowers bloom at the tips of the stems.

RELATED TO RHIPSALIS

Hatiora, Cactus Family

Rhipsalis mesembryanthemoides

Clusters of chubby stems densely packed together, looking adorable. As they grow, they start to droop. In spring, delicate white flowers also bloom. It dislikes strong light. Be mindful not to let water accumulate in the saucer.

Hatiora salicornioides

Also called "Dancing Bones Cactus." Short stems link and branch out while hanging down. It blooms yellow flowers in early summer. Excessive humidity in summer can cause moisture issues.

Crassula, Stonecrop Family

Crassula *'Ivory Pagoda'*

Short leaves covered in fine white hairs grow overlapping each other. They readily produce offsets and form clusters with their peculiar grass-like appearance. Growth is extremely slow. Provide good airflow in summer and water sparingly.

Crassula fusca

With decreasing temperatures, the green leaves turn vivid red in fall. They produce offsets at the base and grow compactly. Water sparingly and expose to sunlight for more vibrant fall colors.

Crassula capitella

The geometric leaves grow densely overlapping like towers. In summer, the green leaves also turn madder red with decreasing temperatures. The white flowers blooming in spring have a pleasant fragrance. It dislikes the summer humidity.

Crassula arborescens

The cute round leaves with red edges and characteristic spots are prominent. They grow into sizable plants with a woody stem. Exposure to cold turns the green leaves pinkish-red in fall. Be cautious of direct sunlight in summer and frost in winter.

Crassula volkensii

Small leaves with magenta spots extend branches in all directions. The lush green leaves in summer turn reddish in fall with decreasing temperatures. White flowers bloom in spring. It's sensitive to cold, requiring at least 50°F (10°C).

Crassula ovata f. variegata

A variegated variety of the jade plant. The white variegated parts turn pink during the fall foliage period. When it grows taller, prune it back in spring for propagation.

Crassula *'Moonglow'*

It unfolds triangular leaves alternately, growing upward like a tower, showcasing a solid presence. The leaves are densely covered in fuzz, giving a matte texture. Ensure good airflow to prevent moisture buildup, especially in summer.

Crassula cooperi

The upper side of the green leaves has red spots, while the underside is reddish-brown, forming small clusters. The cute pink flowers bloom from early summer to summer. It's sensitive to excessive humidity, preferring slightly dry conditions.

Crassula clavata

The strikingly red, fleshy leaves make a strong impression. Native to South Africa. Flowering occurs in early spring. From fall to spring, exposing it to sunlight will enhance its vibrant colors. It's prolific, so it can be pruned and propagated in the spring growing season.

Crassula *'Tom Thumb'*
Small triangular leaves are alternately stacked in this dwarf species. It branches well and readily forms clusters. The red foliage along the edges of the green leaves is also beautiful.

Crassula cordata
The fluttery, curled leaves are unique, giving the plant a lively appearance. In early spring, tiny flowers bloom on elongated stems. During the fall foliage period, the leaves turn pink, adding a charming touch.

Crassula perforata
Also called "String of Buttons," it's a spreading variety that grows like a tower of lime green triangular leaves alternately stacked. The edges of the leaves turn pink during the fall foliage period. It's not prone to branching. Be cautious of high temperatures and humidity in summer.

Crassula perfoliata var. falcata
With large, sword-shaped leaves alternating from side to side, it grows upward. Native to South Africa, when mature, it may produce offsets from the sides. Winter management requires indoor temperatures above 37°F (3°C).

Crassula turrita
Unique with overlapping yellow-green triangular leaves, it tends to lift during the growing season. If you want to keep it compact, consider pruning. It doesn't undergo much fall coloration.

Crassula arta
It grows upward with symmetrical white leaves, lending it the nickname "Alabaster Towers." It dislikes summer humidity and heat, so manage it in partial shade during summer. Winter temperatures should be above 37°F (3°C).

Crassula schmidtii
The sharp, elongated green leaves turn a deep, rich red, creating a stunning display. As it grows, it becomes more dynamic. Pink flowers bloom in summer. Pruning the flower stems from the base encourages new growth.

Crassula punctulata
Its delicate appearance comes from the little silver-green leaves growing and branching upward, forming clusters. Be mindful of summer humidity. It's hardy and can tolerate outdoor conditions down to -30° to -35°F (-1° to -2°C).

Crassula americana cv. *'Flame'*
The leaves spread out like a cross, lime green in summer and vivid red in winter. The intense red foliage, as the name suggests, resembles flames. It's resilient to both heat and cold and can be overwintered outdoors in regions other than cold climates.

Crassula americana cv. *'Flame'* **var.**

Ivory-colored spots adorn the yellow-green leaves like a border. In winter, the variegated parts turn pink, creating a vibrant display. It's tolerant to dry conditions, so watering should be moderate.

Crassula undulatafolia

Also called "Ripple Jade," its grass-like appearance with wavy ribbons is eye-catching. It grows upright and bushy. As it gets colder, the edges of the leaves turn red like fall leaves.

Crassula expansa ssp. fragilis

Its charming small round leaves spread vigorously sideways. The contrast between the green leaves and red stems is beautiful. During midsummer, place it in partial shade to prevent leaf scorch. It has moderate cold resistance.

Crassula radicans

The green leaves turn bright red as the temperature drops. In spring, it sends up red flower stems with white blooms. It's especially beautiful when grown in clusters. With proper frost protection, it can withstand cold temperatures.

Crassula pellucida

It spreads horizontally like a groundcover while growing. The pinkish underside of the leaves gives the impression of a border on the variegated leaves. As it gets colder, it turns reddish-purple throughout. It's resilient to both heat and cold.

Crassula conjuncta

Also known as "Ivory Towers," it appears as a stack of compact rosettes. From fall, the leaf tips turn red. New shoots emerge from the base and spread out. It's tolerant to dry conditions.

Crassula ovata *'Hobbit'*

With leaves resembling donkey ears, it grows upright into a shrub. As the temperature drops, the green leaves take on a yellowish tint, and the tips turn red. It's a summer variety of the jade plant and should be kept indoors in winter.

Crassula *'Jade Necklace'*

Its thick leaves grow upward in an alternating pattern, giving it a unique appearance. When the weather gets cold, the leaf edges turn red. In summer, keep it in bright, well-ventilated shade. It's sensitive to excessive moisture and can be propagated through cuttings.

Crassula perforata f. variegata

A variegated variety of "String of Buttons." Cream-colored spots border the green leaves widely. When exposed to cold, they turn pink from the edges. During midsummer, keep it in partial shade. It can be propagated through cuttings.

Crassula muscosa

A variety with a number of nicknames including "Lizard's Tail" due to its densely stacked small, hard triangular leaves. When it grows larger, it produces offsets from between the leaves. Strong sunlight can cause leaf scorching.

Crassula *'Momiji Matsuri'*

"Momiji" is the word for the red of maple leaves heralding the start of fall. The fiery leaves of this variety leaves are elongated and arranged in a regular pattern compared. The stunning color emerges as temperatures drop. It stays green during summer. It can overwinter outdoors if not in a cold region.

Crassula rupestris

Cross-stacked lime-green leaves with a white powdery coating grow upward and naturally branch out as they grow. It blooms small flowers in early spring. Prune back when it becomes too elongated.

Crassula remota

Almond-shaped small silver leaves with white fuzz turn reddish-purple as it gets colder. It branches well and grows prostrate. It can even be allowed to cascade from the edges of pots.

Crassula rogersii

With rugby ball-shaped, plump leaves. It turns vivid yellow in winter, with the tips and stems becoming bright red. Enjoys sunlight but needs protection from leaf scorch in summer. Keep in temperatures above 41°F (5°C) in winter.

Crassula *'Morgan's Beauty'*

Circular silver leaves are layered outwards in all directions, forming a fascinating stacked appearance. It offsets and grows compactly. It dislikes excess moisture and is suited for winter conditions. Gloriously pink flower clusters bloom from winter into spring. Avoid exposing it to rain.

A RELATIVE OF CRASSULA

Crassulaceae, Genus: Crassula

Crassula lycopodioides var. pseudolycopodioides

Its scale-like small leaves are beautifully stacked, growing slender and upright. If left unattended, it gracefully droops its branches. Resilient to heat, cold, and drought but avoid frost.

Crassula atropurpurea var. watermeyeri

Oval green leaves covered in hair-like fuzz turn a subdued red in fall. It grows with branches reaching upward and outwards. Prune if it grows too long, and use those cuttings for propagation.

Sinocrassula densirosulata

Its rounded small leaves turn orange-tinted when they undergo fall coloration. It grows slowly, producing side shoots and forming clusters. It's sturdy and easy to care for. In summer, provide partial shade and keep the soil slightly dry.

Aeonium, Family: Crassulaceae, Genus: Aeonium

Aeonium arboreum *'Velour'*

The large, rounded rosettes formed by its leaves exude a powerful and outstanding presence. It branches well, forming voluminous plants. It turns a beautiful reddish-brown in winter.

Aeonium arboreum *'Zwartkop'*

Its glossy black rosette-shaped leaves have a charm reminiscent of black roses. It's a representative species of Aeonium. As it grows upright, prune back to maintain its shape. In winter, keep it indoors in a sunny spot.

Aeonium sedifolium

Clustered short leaves resemble grains of rice. The red lines on the green leaves are also striking. As it grows, the stems become bushy and compact. During the fall coloration period, even the green leaves turn orange.

Aeonium tabuliforme var. minima

A rare type where green leaves with fine hairs overlap and spread out flatly. It produces offsets well at the base, allowing for propagation through division. It dislikes excessive moisture, so ensure good airflow. It doesn't undergo fall coloration.

Aeonium arboreum var. rubrolineatum

Its long, slender brown leaves adorned with dark purple blotches are exquisite. During the summer dormant period, these striped patterns become prominent. As it grows, it becomes tall and erect. Avoid direct sunlight in summer.

Aeonium haworthii *'Tricolor'*

In winter, the leaf edges are vivid red, and new shoots take on a yellowish tint. It readily produces offsets and undergoes intricate branching. Growth halts and it enters dormancy in summer. Avoid excessive moisture and keep it in partial shade.

RELATED TO AEONIUM

Aichryson, Family: Crassulaceae, Genus: Aichryson

Aichryson x domesticum *'Variegata'*

Its refreshing contrast between pale yellow-green variegation and vibrant green leaves makes it a popular variety. It's sensitive to both excess moisture and cold. Provide partial shade in summer to prevent leaf scorch and keep indoors in sunny spots during winter.

Aichryson *'Lemonade'*

Its short-haired, refreshing green leaves feel sticky to the touch. Its well-formed rosette shape is visually appealing. It grows upright with a compact form. It dislikes high temperatures and humidity. In winter, it turns yellowish-red.

Cotyledon, Family: Crassulaceae, Genus: Cotyledon

Cotyledon orbiculate

Its thick, large leaves are covered in a white powder, creating a beautiful contrast with the red edges. During the fall coloration period, the leaf tips turn even more vibrant red. It grows quickly and can become a large plant in just a few years. It's easy to care for.

Cotyledon undulata

The fan-shaped leaves with frilly edges are silvery-gray and large, adorned with a white powder. Since the powder can rub off, avoid getting water on the leaves. It dislikes high temperatures and humidity. Provide shade in summer and keep the soil slightly dry.

Cotyledon tomentosa ssp. ladismithensis

The thick leaves, covered in fuzz, have serrated protrusions at their tips, resembling a bear cub's paw. During fall, the redness at the tips intensifies. As it grows, the stems become erect. It may drop leaves due to heat.

Cotyledon ladismithiensis f. variegata

It has white and yellow variegation, with the white variegation being more delicate. In summer, provide shade and good airflow while keeping the soil slightly dry.

Cotyledon elisae

The red lines bordering the green leaves are beautiful, and during fall, they become richly vivid. The bell-shaped orange to red flowers blooming from May to July are also charming. It grows slowly, reaching upward.

Cotyledon orbiculata *'Oophylla'*

Its slender leaves are coated in white powder, with red coloring along the edges. They grow upward. When exposed to rain, the white powder may wash off, leaving black spots. Avoid strong sunlight and keep the soil slightly dry.

Cotyledon orbiculata *'Fukkura'*

The plump leaves blow a white powder, with faint red lines visible along the edges. It's prone to elongation, so ensure it gets plenty of sunlight. Watch out for leaf scorch in summer.

Cotyledon macrantha var. virescens

The large oval leaves with red borders are eye-catching. As the temperature drops, they turn even more vibrant red. It grows vigorously, becoming a large-sized species with offspring emerging from the base. Provide partial shade in midsummer.

Cotyledon pendens

Its round, small leaves are cute and spread out like a creeper. Enjoy letting it cascade from the pot. Avoid strong light and prolonged rain. If the leaves turn yellow, it's a sign of needing fertilizer.

Graptopetalum, Crassulaceae, Graptopetalum Genus

Graptopetalum paraguayense

As it grows, it forms rosette-shaped stems with branches extending in all directions. In cold weather, the leaves take on a pale pink color. It can also be planted in the ground in regions west of the Kanto area. Propagation through leaf cuttings is also easy.

Graptopetalum *'Daruma Shuurei'*

The delicate mix of light pink and purple is charming. During the fall, the pink color intensifies. The stems grow upward, and leaves are densely packed on the upper part, making it a great choice for mass planting. Be cautious of leaf scorching during the summer.

Graptopetalum mendozae

The rosettes formed by small leaves resemble tiny flowers. They grow in clusters. This popular variety turns a lovely pink in the fall, but its leaves are easily detached, so handle with care. It's cold-resistant and can be pruned if it becomes unruly.

GRAPTOPETALUM-SEDUM HYBRIDS Graptosedum, Crassulaceae, Graptosedum Genus

Graptosedum *'Francesco Baldi'*

It grows gracefully with slender leaves radiating outwards. During the fall season, the light blue leaves take on a pinkish hue, creating a vibrant appearance. It forms a clump and is cold-resistant, able to survive winters above 32°F (0°C).

Graptosedum *'Bronze'*

A representative species of the copper-leaved varieties. In winter, it transforms into a subdued reddish-brown. You can enjoy its natural growth form without pruning. It produces yellow flowers in spring. It's easy to care for and propagate.

Graptosedum *'Little Gem'*

The subdued green leaf color turns reddish-brown in winter. The yellow flowers that bloom in spring add a touch of elegance to the remaining red leaves. Its growth is slow, and it doesn't tolerate heat well.

GRAPTOPETALUM-ECHEVERIA HYBRIDS Graptoveria, a Hybrid of Graptopetalum and Echeveria

Graptoveria *'A Grim One'*

The slightly pink-tipped ends of its yellowish leaves provide are anything but grim. It grows in clusters, with offsets appearing around the parent plant. It's relatively cold-resistant. It produces yellow flowers in spring.

Graptoveria *'Purple King'*

It has a texture resembling white powder, and during winter, it turns a vivid pink. Its cute yellow flowers in spring add to its charm. While it's sensitive to heat, it's relatively cold-resistant.

Graptoveria *'Mrs. Richards'*

Its elegant, pale purple-pink leaves with a white powdery texture are eye-catching. As it grows, it forms an upright stem, and during the fall foliage period, the pink becomes more intense, giving it a glossy appearance. If it grows tall and the plant becomes unruly, you can prune it.

Pachyphytum, Crassulaceae, Pachyphytum Genus

Pachyphytum *'Koubijin'*

A Japanese variety also known as "Kyoto Beauty." Its thick, elongated leaves point upward and turn pink at lower temperatures. Since they have a white powdery coating, it's advisable to water the soil rather than the leaves.

Pachyphytum *'Gekkabijin'*

A Japanese variety meaning "Moon Flower Beauty," it has cute, slender leaves that tend to cluster. Its elegant powder-blue hue turns reddish at lower temperatures. Be particularly cautious during humid summers. Pruning can encourage the growth of offsets at the base.

Pachyphytum compactum

Leaves resembling shaved polyhedrons are unique. They grow densely together in clusters. White veins appear on the leaves during growth. During the fall season, they turn yellow to orange. They are relatively resistant to cold temperatures.

Pachyphytum oviferum *'Tsukibijin'*

Rounded and chubby leaves with a charming appearance, with a hint of purple at the tips. When it undergoes fall foliage, the entire plant turns pink. If it grows too tall, you can trim it back. During summer, keep it in semi-shade and water sparingly.

Pachyphytum hookeri

Thick leaves with a white powdery coating turn purple during fall, creating an enchanting atmosphere. Avoid touching the leaves as the powder can rub off. It's a robust and easy-to-care-for plant that can be propagated through stem and leaf cuttings.

Pachyphytum oviferum *'Momobijin'*

Rounded, plump leaves with gentle pink tips, which become more vibrant as temperatures drop. During summer, it should be kept in bright, well-ventilated, semi-shaded areas with slightly dry conditions.

PACHYPHYTUM-ECHEVERIA HYBRIDS

Pachyveria, Genus Pachyveria, Family Crassulaceae Compactum

Pachyphytum uniflorum

Spreading rosettes formed by wide, pointed leaves create a vibrant look. It turns purple during the fall season. It doesn't tolerate high temperatures and humidity during summer. In summer, keep it in semi-shade with good airflow. Insufficient sunlight can lead to elongation.

Pachyveria *'Blue Mist'*

Unique, faceted leaves resembling cut surfaces that cluster densely. White stripes may appear on the leaves during growth. During fall, they turn yellow to orange. It's relatively cold-resistant.

Pachyveria hialium

Striking, thick leaves with pointed tips. In summer, the silver-blue leaf color turns pink with lower temperatures. The stems stand upright, and offsets appear at the base. It can be propagated through stem and leaf cuttings.

Sempervivum Genus, Crassulaceae Family

Sempervivum *'Aldo Moro'*

This variety has dark green leaves with dark red-purple edges and undersides. As the temperature drops in fall, the entire plant turns a deep red-purple color. It can be divided and propagated through offsets in spring and fall.

Sempervivum *'Gazelle'*

This variety features vibrant green leaves with white threads that emerge from the leaf tips and cover the entire plant. When the temperature decreases, the undersides of the leaves turn red-purple. It produces offsets easily and forms attractive clusters.

Sempervivum arachnoideum *'Cobweb Joy'*

The name "cobweb" refers to the white threads covering the plant. It has slightly shorter leaves stacked in abundance. In fall and winter, it turns a beautiful red color. It readily produces offsets.

Sempervivum *'Sakai'*

This variety has a two-tone coloration with green upper leaf surfaces and red-purple undersides. The edges of the leaves are covered in delicate, hair-like fuzz. During the fall foliage season, the entire plant turns a bright red-purple.

Sempervivum *'Sprite'*

The lime green leaves turn red from the outermost leaves inward as the temperature drops, ultimately becoming entirely red. It produces offsets continuously and forms clusters. It thrives with minimal watering during summer.

Sempervivum tectorum *'Red Purple'*

This variety is characterized by its long, sharp leaves, giving it a refined appearance. The grayish velvety green leaves gradually turn red-purple with the onset of fall. It can be divided and propagated through offsets in spring and fall.

Sempervivum *'Black Mini'*

The pointed chocolate-colored leaves give this variety a chic and elegant look. When it gets cold, the color deepens, approaching black. It thrives in well-lit and well-ventilated locations.

Sempervivum *'Bronco'*

During winter, it exhibits a deep wine-red coloration. As spring arrives, it gradually transitions to green, creating a striking contrast between green and bronze-tipped leaves. It readily produces offsets and forms clusters.

Sempervivum *'More Honey'*

In summer, it has a refreshing light green leaf color, but as temperatures drop in fall, both the undersides and leaf tips turn reddish-brown. During summer, it benefits from partial shade and reduced watering.

Senecio, Asteraceae, Senecio Genus

Senecio herreanus

A summer type also known as "String of Watermelons" owing to the shape of the leaves and their vertical stripes. Its thick stems cascade gracefully, making it quite striking. Pruned branches can be placed on top of soil to root.

Senecio haworthii

This variety's long, slender leaves covered in white fuzz are soft and delicate. The leaves point upward with a slight tip. During summer, avoid direct sunlight and reduce watering. Trim if it becomes too leggy.

Senecio rowleyanus

A much loved variety. Often called "String of Pearls," its spherical leaves are perfect for hanging pots. Keep it away from direct sunlight in summer. Placing branches on soil can promote rooting.

Senecio scaposus

This unusual plant has cylindrical green leaves covered with white fibers resembling Japanese paper. Be careful, as touching the leaves may cause them to shed. Avoid exposing it to rain. Keep it indoors during winter at temperatures above 41°F (5°C).

Senecio 'Peach Necklace'

This variety's slightly pointed leaves resemble peaches. Continuous exposure to direct sunlight can lead to leaf scorching, so provide some shade. It's sensitive to overwatering, so keep it on the drier side. It can produce delicate flowers in spring.

Senecio kleiniiformis

The leaves have distinctive serrations at the tips, resembling arrowheads. When kept on the drier side, the leaves tend to be shorter. During summer, place it in partial shade, and in winter, move it to a well-lit indoor location.

CLOSELY RELATED TO SENECIO

Othonna, a genus in the Asteraceae family

Senecio radicans

Its crescent-shaped leaves are arranged on slender stems, trailing and forming a dynamic appearance. The leaf tips point upward, adding a sense of movement. Protect it from frost as it can damage the leaves during winter. In winter, bring it indoors.

Othonna capensis

Its slender stems bear oval green leaves, creating a cascading and beautiful look. Yellow flowers bloom in spring. Manage it with slightly dry conditions and avoid strong sunlight in summer. The leaves turn reddish in the cold.

Othonna capensis 'Ruby Necklace'

This variety turns purple when it matures, and its cascading appearance is graceful. Delicate yellow flowers bloom in spring. Protect it from frost and cold winds during winter, keeping it slightly dry indoors.

"Books to Span the East and West"

Tuttle Publishing was founded in 1832 in the small New England town of Rutland, Vermont [USA]. Our core values remain as strong today as they were then—to publish best-in-class books which bring people together one page at a time. In 1948, we established a publishing outpost in Japan—and Tuttle is now a leader in publishing English-language books about the arts, languages and cultures of Asia. The world has become a much smaller place today and Asia's economic and cultural influence has grown. Yet the need for meaningful dialogue and information about this diverse region has never been greater. Over the past seven decades, Tuttle has published thousands of books on subjects ranging from martial arts and paper crafts to language learning and literature—and our talented authors, illustrators, designers and photographers have won many prestigious awards. We welcome you to explore the wealth of information available on Asia at **www.tuttlepublishing.com**.

Published by Tuttle Publishing, an imprint of Periplus Editions (HK) Ltd.

www.tuttlepublishing.com

TANIKUSHOKUBUTSU START BOOK
© Kentaro Kuroda 2021
English translation rights arranged with IE-NO-HIKARI ASSOCIATION though Japan UNI Agency, Inc., Tokyo

English Translation © 2024 by Periplus Editions (HK) Ltd. Tuttle Publishing has altered and/or added images and information on pages 12 and 80 of the English edition.

ISBN 978-0-8048-5600-3

Staff of Japanese Edition:
Publisher: Kawachi Naoyuki **Printing and Binding:** Toshoinsatsu Co., Ltd. **Book Design:** Fujita Kohei (Barber) **Photography:** Takashi Matsumura Toyoa Miyako (pages 64–80) **Research:** Hiromi Yamamoto **Proof Reading:** K's Office **DTP Production:** Tenryusha **Editing:** Ayako Hirotani

Distributed by

North America, Latin America & Europe
Tuttle Publishing
364 Innovation Drive
North Clarendon, VT 05759-9436 U.S.A.
Tel: 1 (802) 773-8930
Fax: 1 (802) 773-6993
info@tuttlepublishing.com
www.tuttlepublishing.com

Asia Pacific
Berkeley Books Pte. Ltd.
3 Kallang Sector #04-01
Singapore 349278
Tel: (65) 6741 2178
Fax: (65) 6741 2179
inquiries@periplus.com.sg
www.tuttlepublishing.com

28 27 26 25 24
10 9 8 7 6 5 4 3 2 1

Printed in China
2409EP